Go Back To School

I will instruct you and teach you in the way you should go;
I will counsel you with my loving eye on you.

—Psalm 32:8

(El-Roi) The God Who Sees

Lisa Ulmer

ISBN 978-1-64258-578-0 (paperback)
ISBN 978-1-64258-589-6 (hardcover)
ISBN 978-1-64258-579-7 (digital)

Christian Faith Publishing, Inc.
832 Park Avenue
Meadville, PA 16335
www.christianfaithpublishing.com

Printed in the United States of America

Respectfully and lovingly dedicated to my deceased
grandfather, Rev. John Frank Ulmer, who fought the good
fight of faith and completed his kingdom assignment
up until the age of 101, who shaped my spiritually
foundation as a young child. I say, "Thank you, Daddy."

To. Nina

My future partner
in writing . . .

Love You

[signature]

Table of Contents

Lesson I

Handcrafted by God

"All scripture is given by inspiration of God, and is profitable
for doctrine, for reproof, for correction, for instruction in
righteousness, that the man of God may be complete, thoroughly
equipped for every good work." (2 Timothy 3:16–17)

(Jehovah - M'Kaddesh) The Lord Who Sanctifies Me

Introduction:

Isn't it ironic that as parents or adults, we inquire from children as young as four or five years of age who they want to be when they grow up? Subconsciously, children begin to formulate seeds of identity in the blueprints of their minds at such a premature age. And this is why children will choose the career of a parent, other relatives, or what they see on television because children identify themselves with what's in their environment or surroundings.

As adults, do we do this because of fear? Fear of not knowing what lies ahead of us? Whatever the reason, it's of no importance. What's significant and will transform our life and make a difference in the lives of children is for everyone to know who they are in the kingdom of the almighty, all-knowing, loving God, Abba, Father. We must first start by seeking the kingdom of God, "and all things will work together for our good; because we have already been called according to his purpose."

"Start children on the way they should go, and even when they are old they will not turn from it." (Prov. 22:6)

Abba – I belong to you.

Objective:

"Yet you, Lord, are our Father. We are the clay, you are the potter; we are all the work of your hand" (Isa. 64:8).

Mission:

"And He made from one man every nation to live on all the face of the earth, having determined their appointed times and the boundaries of their habitation" (Acts 17:26).

The Search is Over

The search for purpose is dominant amongst the believer as well as the unbeliever. Feelings of emptiness, unfulfillment, or thoughts of there must be more to oneself and/or life itself can consume the soul and ache away at the heart. The scripture in the Book of Jeremiah should be the catalyst of all sermons, branded in hearts, minds, and souls from our childhood into our adult life. We must embrace the truth that we are predestined and come from a higher power in heavenly places. God speaks and reveals to Jeremiah the *who, what, when*, and *why* of mankind's existence.

Now, let's begin to explore our purpose and destiny from inception to the conception.

"Before I formed you in the womb I knew you, and before you were born I consecrated you; I appointed you as a prophet to the nations" (Jer. 1:4).

In this, twenty-seven worded scripture, *"six things"* take place, and the number six represents man in the kingdom of God (see more Lesson X):

1. **Identity**
2. **Relationship**
3. **Formation**
4. **Consecration**
5. **Purpose**
6. **Assignment**

God reveals to Jeremiah his *identity* and explains that there was a *relationship* between the two of them before He *formed* his embryo in the womb. God then *consecrates* Jeremiah and *assigns* him to his *purpose* for his life on earth, appointing him to be a prophet to the nations.

The same covenant applies to you and me. We were with the Father from the beginning. We had an intimate relationship with Him. The Lord formed us, anointed us, and gave us an assignment to be purposeful. Our purpose is to fulfill the assignment. However, we must first recognize that we are stewards for the kingdom of heaven. This is why scripture tells us to "But seek ye first the kingdom of God, and his righteousness; and all these *things* shall be added onto you." (Matt. 6:33)

When we seek God first, He will restore the six covenant "*things*" in Jeremiah chapter 1.

"And we know that in all *things* God works for the good of those who love him, who have been called according to his purpose." (Rom. 8:28)

God has prepared us for our purpose. "For we are God's handiwork, created in Christ Jesus to do good works, which God prepared in advance for us to do" (Eph. 2:10).

Take a look at how King David in the Book of Psalms graciously expounds on God's divine craftsmanship in creating mankind:

> "You fashioned my inner most being, you knit me together in my mother's womb. I thank you cause I'm awesomely made, wonderfully; your works are wonders I know this very well. My bones were not hidden from you, when I was being made in secrete. Intricately woven in the depths of the earth, Your eye could see me as an embryo, But in your book all my days had been shaped before any of them existed." (Ps. 139:13–16)

Process It

Did you process that? Let's read the last verse again: "All the days ordained for me were written in your book; before one of them came to be."

God saw the finished work in us before we were even born. *Imagine that!*

We Are Uniquely Crafted in the Blood

On the average, there are over one hundred thousand strands of hair on a young adult, and the hair root is below the scalp and is enclosed in a hair follicle which connects to our bloodstream. And God said, "Indeed, the very hairs of your head are all numbered. Don't be afraid; you are worth more than many sparrows" (Luke 12:7).

Our DNA links us to our genetic growth, development, functioning, and reproduction of all known living organisms; it's all in the blood.

It's Generational

There are three types of DNA testing hair strands:

1. Y-DNA—testing the male gender–linked Y-chromosome for information passed in a direct line from father to son.
2. Autosomal DNA or (at DNA)—tests DNA from all of the chromosomes except gender-linked X and Y. This test links cousins across gender.
3. Mitochondria is the direct female line from mother to child; only passed on by a daughter.

The Twin Factor

Identical twin embryos share virtually their entire DNA. During early fetal development, however, identical twins undergo more than three hundred genetic mutations, or copy errors, on average. As human cells divide trillions of times during a lifespan, a few hundred genetic mutations could lead to millions and trillions of genetic differences in the DNA of identical twins over the years. Therefore, twins have the same genes, so they generally look alike and are the same sex; but they distinctively possess their own uniqueness.

Genesis 2:7

Scripture: "And the Lord God formed man of the dust of the ground, and breathed into his nostrils the breath of life; and man became a living soul."

One Nation Under God

We are all woven together in the kingdom of God by Christ Jesus—strand by strand—from our parents down to our ancestors; but we possess our own body, soul, and spirit, individually created in God's love.

> "Remember the former things, those of long
> ago, I am God, and there is no other; I am God
> and there is none like me. I make known the end
> from the beginning, from ancient times, what is
> still to come. I say, "My purpose will stand, and I
> will do all that I please." (Isa. 46:9–10)

Psalms 145:13

Scripture: "Your kingdom is an everlasting kingdom, and your dominion endures through all generations."

Lesson II

Mankind the Trifecta

"It is I who made the earth, and created man upon
it I stretched out the heavens with My hands and
I ordained all their host." Isaiah 45:12

(Elohim) God Our Creator

Introduction:

In the Book of John chapter one, God places His Word at the forefront of all things He created. God makes it clear to us in this scripture that the Word has life and the Word produced all things through Him as He spoke it into existence. God said, "In the beginning was the *Word,* and the *Word* was with *God,* and the *Word* was *God.* He was with God in the beginning. "Through him all things were made; without him nothing was made that has been made. In *him* was *life,* and that *life* was the *light of all mankind."* (John 1:1–2)

Who is God talking about? God is talking about *Jesus, you,* and *I. Jesus* is the *life* and *light of mankind* from the beginning before God created the earth.

John 10:28–30

"I give them eternal life, and they shall never perish; no one will snatch them out of my hand. My father, who has given them to me, is greater than all; no one can snatch them out of my Father's hand. I and the Father are one."

Objective:

"In the beginning was the Word, and the Word was with God, and the Word was God. He was with God in the beginning. Through him all things were made; without him nothing was made that has been made. In him was *life,* and that *life* was the *light* of all *mankind."* (John 1:1–2)

Mission:

Then Jesus again spoke to them, saying, "I am the *Light* of the world; he who follows me will not walk in the darkness, but will have the *Light* of *life."* (John 8:12)

Graphed in from the Beginning

In the compare-and-contrast chart below, we see the function, similarities, and differences in the kingdom of God and mankind intricately intertwined together.

- ➤ the hierarchy God's Word
- ➤ the Trinity of God: Father, Son, Holy Spirit
- ➤ the Triune of mankind; body, soul, spirit, in the likeness of the Trinity
- ➤ the covenant between mankind and the kingdom; Jesus the sacrificial Lamb
- ➤ the blood seat of mercy and grace: redemption

Compare and Contrast

Similarities

Differences

Differences		Similarities		Differences
Body Five Senses of Man		The Word of God		Father Creator of Man
Soul Character of Man	Man	God	Kingdom of God	Son Redeemer of Man
Spirit Heart of Man		Holy Ghost		Holy Ghost Guider of Man
		Jesus		
		The Blood		

Trifecta of Mankind: God's Masterpiece

Then God said, "Let us make mankind in our image" (Gen. 1:26). The souls of mankind unified with the Trinity of God through His Word and metamorphosed into a trifecta. The Trinity of God transcended the souls of mankind into a triune—body, soul, and spirit; and now we see mankind functioning like God, three parts as one. Created in the image of God, man is likewise a trinity. He has a spiritual nature that is separate and distinct from the body in which it dwells. The outer circle stands for the body of man, the middle circle for the soul, and the inner for the Spirit.

Truine—consisting of three in one.

Genesis 1:26

Scripture: "Then God said, 'Let us make man in Our image according to Our likeness; and let them rule over the fish of the sea and over the birds of the sky and over the cattle and over all the earth, and over every creeping thing that creeps on the earth.'"

Man the Body

The Body is stimulated by the five senses: Sight, Smell, Hearing, Tactile, and Taste.

2 Corinthians 4:16

Scripture: "The body is the outer man connected to the material things in life. Therefore, we do not lose heart. Though outwardly we are wasting away, yet inwardly we are being renewed day by day."

Man the Soul

The Soul of Man is his Imagination, Conscious, Memory, Reasoning, and Affection.

3 John 1:2

Scripture: "Beloved, I pray that all may go well with you and that you may be in good health, as it goes well with your soul."

Man the Spirit

The Spirit of Man is his Faith, Hope, Reverence, Prayer, and Worship.

Lehman Strauss

John 4:24
Scripture: "For God is a Spirit; and they that worship must worship him in spirit and in truth."

The Love Connection

➤ There is absolutely no way to sum up who God is in just a few words because God is His Word (John 1:1). "In him we move and we live and we have our being" (Acts 17:28). God loves us so much that He created us in His image a triune. God said, "Let us make man in our image." What is the image of God? The Trinity. God even created a heaven for us called the Garden of Eden for mankind to have dominion, subdue, and replenish the earth.

➤ The covenant was set: the Trinity of God in heaven and the Triune of Man on earth joined together in the supernatural image and Spirit of God Himself. "I have made heaven, the men and the beast which are on the face of the earth My great power and by My outstretched arm, and I will give it to the one who is pleasing in My sight" (Jer. 27:5). The Lord has given us His infinite power by His Word, dominion and authority by His Son's precious blood, and His anointing the Holy Ghost to lead and guide us.

John1:14
Scripture: "The Word became flesh and made his dwelling among us. We have seen his glory, the glory of the one and only Son, who came from the Father, full of grace and truth."

Lesson III

The Blood

"But when they came to Jesus and found that he was already dead, they did not break his legs. Instead, one of the soldiers pierced Jesus' side with a spear, bringing a sudden flow of blood and water." (John 19:33–34)

(Jehovah – Mephalti) My Deliverer

Introduction:

The Blood of Jesus Christ is absolutely the most precious act of God, offered to redeem mankind, our fate sealed in the Blood.

Who—Jesus Christ of Nazareth the Messiah

What—Jesus Christ was crucified; He sacrificed and shed His blood in seven places

When—About 2,000 years ago

Where—In Jerusalem, in a place called Golgotha (which means, "the place of the skulls"), Mt. Calvary

Why—To redeem you and me from our sins and make us "at-one" with the Father again.

Objective:

"I am being spiritually healed; one day even my flesh will be replaced with an incorruptible body . . . who Himself bore our sins in His own body on the tree, that we, having died to sin, might live for righteous by whose stripes you were healed" (1 Pet. 2:24).

(Jehovah Rapha) The Lord Who Heals

Mission:

"Having therefore, brethren, boldness to enter into the holiest by the Blood of Jesus, By a new and living way, which he hath consecrated for us, through the veil, that is to say, his flesh; And having an high priest over the house of God; Let us draw near with a true heart in full assurance of faith, having our hearts sprinkled from an evil conscience, and our bodies washed with pure water." (Heb. 10:19–22)

od of Jesus: What Does It Mean?

Blood of Jesus is the foundation of redemption. Jesus Christ died on the cross, shedding His blood (and was resurrected) as the only acceptable payment for our sins. The disciple Peter wrote in 1 Peter 1: 18–20, "For you know that it was not with perishable things such as silver or gold that you were redeemed from the empty way of life you inherited from your forefathers, but with the precious blood of Christ, a lamb without blemish or spot. He was known before the foundation of the world, but was revealed in the last times for your sake."

Every human born has sinned against God and fallen short of His standard (Rom. 3:23). We do not and cannot earn salvation by keeping the Old Testament Law or by simply being a good person. We will fail every time; it is in our nature to sin. It is only through sacrificing His Son Jesus in our place that we can acquire complete forgiveness. We can all attain this by accepting Jesus as our Savior and accepting that He shed His blood to atone for the sins of all who repent. The act of communion does not save us, but we honor this wonderful gift from God with communion as a way to remember His sacrifice.

Blood of Jesus: Why Is This Required?

In the Old Testament, after Adam's original sin, God accepted the death of an animal as a substitute for the sinner. The animal's shed blood was proof that one life had to be given for another. Life is precious, and God places great value on each one of His beings. This agreement demonstrated that, while blood symbolizes death, it also showed that a life was spared. However, this was a temporary covenant. This blood needed to be repeated daily and yearly. God would later send His only begotten Son providing a new covenant, or New Testament, through Jesus Christ. Jesus would die in place of all sinners. His sacrifice fulfilled completely what the Old Testament covenant could not do. His blood would remove the sins from the world for all who put their faith in Him. This sacrifice would never have to be repeated; it is an eternal covenant.

Blood of Jesus: How Is This Possible?

It is possible for everyone to have the protection and forgiveness that the Blood of Jesus provides. Regardless of what sins and offenses we have committed against God, He offers this gift to each of us. John 3:17 tells us that Jesus didn't come to condemn us but to save us.

It is not enough to say we believe in God or know about Him. We must want to know Him personally and accept the sacrifice of His Son, Jesus, to receive it. The Bible, God's Word, says that no one can enter heaven or get to the Father except through the Son (John 14:6). And in John 6:40, Jesus says all who believe in Him will receive everlasting life with Him! We are only asked to believe (have faith), confess Him, and transfer ownership of our lives to Him. If you have never asked Jesus into your life, won't you ask Him now? If you truly believe and trust this in your heart, receiving Jesus alone as your Savior, declaring, "Jesus is Lord," you will be saved from judgment and spend eternity in heaven.

AllAboutGod

Sinner's Prayer (Read Aloud)

Father, I come to You surrendering all that I am, and all that I have. I believe with all of my heart, all of my soul, and all of my mind that Jesus Christ died for my sins and He rose again. Lord, I accept Your only begotten Son, Jesus Christ, as my personal Savior.

Welcome to the kingdom of God. You are saved!

Jesus' Blood Perfected Us!

> "Then He said to them, 'This is what is written: the Christ will suffer and rise from the dead on the third day, and in His name repentance and forgiveness of sins will be proclaimed to all nations, beginning in Jerusalem." (Luke 24:46–47)

> "The final act of public expiation has been made on my behalf: For the life of a creature is in the blood, and I have given it to you to make atonement for yourselves on the altar; it is the blood that makes the atonement for one's life." (Lev. 17:11)

The Blood of Jesus shed seven times and seven ways for you and I:

1. Freedom

Jesus shed His blood in the Garden of Gethsemane to redeem our will.

"And he went a little farther, and fell on his face, and prayed, saying O my father, if it be possible, let this bitter cup pass from me; nevertheless not as I will, but thou will" (Matt. 26:39).

2. Healing

Jesus was whipped to break the curse of sickness and disease from our life.

"Who his own self bare our sins in his own body on the tree, that we, being dead to sins, should live onto righteousness: by whose stripes ye were healed" (1 Pet. 2:24).

3. Prosperity

The crown of thorns was placed on Jesus' brow to break the curse of poverty and release us into God's abundance.

"Cursed is the ground for thy sake; in sorrow shalt thou eat of it all the days of thou life; thorns also and thistles shall it bring fourth to thee" (Gen. 3:17–18).

"Christ hath redeemed us from the curse of the law; being made a curse for us."

4. Dominion

Jesus' hands were pierced by the nails to restore total dominion to the works of our hands.

And to bless all the work of thine hand: and thou shall lend onto many nations; and thou shall not borrow. And the Lord shall make thee the head, and not the tail; and thou shall be above only; and thou shall not be beneath. (Deut. 28:12–13)

5. Authority

Jesus' feet were nailed to the cross to restore total dominion in our walk.

"Every place that the sole of your foot shall tread upon, that have I given unto you" (Josh. 1:3).

6. Peace

The spear was thrust through Jesus' side, showing that He died from a broken heart to heal our broken heart.

"The spirit of the Lord is upon me, because he has anointed me to preach the gospel to the poor; he hath sent me to heal the brokenhearted" (Luke 4:18).

7. Restoration

Jesus bled on the inside when He was bruised to break every iniquity, the inner drive of sin, from my life.

"He was bruised for our iniquities" (Isa. 53:5).

Inspired by: Pastors Larry and Tiz Huch

God's Favoritism for Mankind

God is a gracious gift giver, and He loves flourishing us, His children, with what scriptures describe as the favor of God. The Bible reveals the Lords favor in a multitude of ways; the favor of God is not something we can earn or discern. In the Book of Ephesians, Paul writes and leads us directly to God's divine favor and outstanding grace.

Scripture: "I have gained unmerited favor of God. In Him we have redemption through His blood, the forgiveness of sins, according to the riches of His grace" (Eph. 1:7).

There you have it. There is no greater favor from the Lord than the precious Blood of Jesus. Therefore, God's measure of favor towards mankind, one may say, "seems rare"; but with the blood sacrifice, favor is fair!

Let There Be Light

See Saints, the Blood of Jesus has given us *Freedom, Healing, Prosperity, Dominion, Authority, Peace, and Restoration.* We are free from sin and condemnation; we are not the subordinate. God has made us a kingdom of priest and kings to reign on earth (Rev. 5:10). When fiery trails come our way, we have to renew our minds in the

Word of God and speak positive words over the negative thoughts by casting down imaginations that don't line up with the "blood" sacrifice.

James tells us to "count it all joy." The word *count* means, to add up, tally, and calculate. Well, that means we must add up all of the past trials and tribulations, and remind ourselves that we are overcomers. So when a new trying time shows up, we will trust God to deliver us again, again, and again. Beloved, this is how we begin to move from faith to faith and glory to glory through our trials, which in return bring us treasures.

James 1:3–8 reads, "Knowing that the testing of your faith worketh patience. But let patience have it perfect work, that you may be perfect and complete lacking nothing. If any of you lack wisdom, let him ask of God, who gives to all liberally without reproach, and it will be given to him. But let him ask in faith, without doubting, for he who doubts is like a wave of the sea driven and tossed by the wind. For let no man suppose that he will receive anything from the Lord; he is a double-minded man, unstable in all his ways."

Saints, "All things are possible to him that believes" (Mark 9:23). God says, "And call upon me in the day of trouble: I will deliver you, and you shall honor me" (Ps. 50:15). "Ask and it will be given to you; seek, and you will find; knock, and it will be opened to you. For everyone who asks receives, and the one who seeks finds, and to the one who knocks it will be opened" (Matt. 7:7–8).

We have not because we ask not. Draw near to God, and He will draw near to you. "For I know the plans I have for you," declares the Lord, "plans to prosper you and not harm you, plans to give you hope and a future." (Jer. 29:11)

Gifts of the Spirit

There are nine gifts that the Holy Spirit anoints us with throughout scripture. We see Jesus walking in the Gifts of the

Spirit. The Father has transferred the same anointing to us His children to rule and reign in the Spirit; and to be a witness, spread the gospel, and win souls for the kingdom of heaven. Jesus proclaims,

> "Very truly I tell you, whoever believes in me will do the works I have been doing, and they will do even greater things than these, because I am going to the Father." (John 14:12)
>
> "There are different kinds of gifts, but the same Spirit distributes them. There are different kinds of service, but the same Lord. There are different kinds of working, but in all of them and in everyone it is the same God at work. Now to each one the manifestation of the Spirit is given for the common good. To one there is given through the Spirit a message of wisdom, to another a message of knowledge by means of the same Spirit, to another faith by the same Spirit, to another gifts of healing by that one Spirit, to another miraculous powers, to another prophecy, to another distinguishing between spirits, to another speaking in different kinds of tongues, and to still another the interpretation of tongues. All these are the work of one and the same Spirit, and he distributes them to each one, just as he determines." (1 Cor. 12:4–11)

The gift has already been given. God has given all of His children Gifts of the Spirit to be purposeful and fulfill our calling for His kingdom. We need to ask the Holy Spirit to stir up the gifts within us so we can be prosperous, purposeful, and a blessing to others.

Fruits of the Spirit

"But the fruit of the Spirit is love, joy, peace, longsuffering, kindness, goodness, faithfulness, gentleness and self-control. Against such things there is no law," (Gal. 5:22–23). The Fruits of the Spirit is just as important as the Gifts of the Spirit. To maintain balance in our gifts, we need to be matured, equipped, steadfast, and "*dunamis*" in order to fulfill the fruits of our labor lacking nothing.

Get Connected

Jesus says, "I am the vine, you are the branches. He who abides in Me, and I in him bears much fruit; for without Me you can do nothing." Begin to meditate on His Word, focus on the greater that is in you. If you desire to build upon your gifts, ask God to help you, be still, and listen. "He who humbles himself shall be exalted." (Matt. 23:12)

Blessed be the God and father our Lord Jesus Christ, who has blessed us with every spiritual blessing in the heavenly places in Christ. (Eph. 1:3)

All of God's children have a mountain to be purposeful in, as a steward in the army of the Lord. You just need to log in, change your channel frequency, and don't log out; stay connected and God will reveal Himself. We are not waiting on God; He is waiting on us.

King David in the book of Psalms 121:1 says it like this, "I look onto the hills from which cometh my help, my help comes from the Lord."

Scripture: "How beautiful on the mountains are the feet of those who bring good news, who proclaim peace, who proclaim salvation, who say to Zion, 'Your God reigns!'" (Isa. 52:7)

There are seven mountains that God established for us as His children to rule, reign over, and spread the gospel of Jesus Christ.

The Seven Mountains of Purpose

1. Religion, Five-Fold Ministry: Preacher, Prophet, Teacher, Evangelist, Missionary
2. Family
3. Education
4. Government
5. Media, TV, Screenwriters
6. Arts, Entertainment, Sports
7. Business

To Whom Much is Given Much is Required (Luke 12:36)

Now we know that trials will come to test our faith. God wants us to be steadfast and unmovable in our faith, our purpose, and the journey. First, we must get wisdom and ask the Lord to enlighten our understanding, taking everything to the Lord in prayer. The trials that we may face within the mountains are doctrine, meaning no one on earth is exempt. First Peter 5:9 tells us, "Stand firm against him, and be strong in your faith. Remember that your Christian brothers and sisters all over the world are going through the same kind of suffering you are."

If we can begin to function from our Spirit Man when we are faced with trials and tribulations, we can obtain peace, a peace that surpasses all understanding. Believing without a doubt that "the mountain" shall pass, in due season, we will be victorious. How do we know? Because Jesus shed His blood for our peace; therefore, we need to rest in Him. "So there is a special rest still waiting for the people of God. For all who have entered into God's rest have rested from their labors, just as God did after creating the world. So let us do our best to enter that rest" (Heb. 4:9–11).

Scripture: "Whoever dwells in the shelter of the Most High will rest in the shadow of the Almighty" (Ps. 91:1).

Seventh Heaven

Jesus shed His blood in seven places, and the number seven represents completion and perfection. Jesus completed His purpose on earth with perfection! And He covered us from the crown of heads to the sole of our feet. Therefore, our trials are temporary, not eternal, and we have:

> - *Freedom* to submit any trial to God for His strength and guidance;
> - *Healing* in every area of our bodies and life;
> - *Prosperity* in all that we do;
> - *Dominion* to command those things to be not as though they were;
> - *Authority* because we possess the power;
> - *Peace* that surpasses all understanding, rest in Him;
> - *Restoration,* the ability to return anything back to its former condition.

Be Aware Not Weary

"And let us not be weary in well doing: for in due season we shall reap, if we faint not" (Gal. 6:9).

Below are several areas that trials and trying times may become prevalent in our walk with God, and when they surface, we have to speak to it! "Truly I tell you, if anyone says to this mountain, Go, throw yourself into the sea, and does not doubt in their heart but believes that what they say will happen, it will be done for them" (Mark 11:23). It must obey you! "God's Word does not return unto him void" (Isa. 55:11), and we have sanction to profess the seven places Jesus shed His blood. Over any situation or circumstances, we are triumphant. When seeking out or walking in purpose, things may not always be God-sent, but it can be God-used. Scripture tells us, "But as for you, you meant evil against me; but God meant it for good, in order to bring it about as it is this day, to save many people alive" (Gen. 5:20). God is telling us that He will make all of the bad things, "struggles" we experience good. He will turn them around and make them good, not just for us, but our struggles will be used to be a blessing to others.

The Seven Mountains of Life

Don't assume that just because "something is hard," it's not God's will.

1. Family—growing up, parents, friends
2. Work—purpose, job, business
3. Financial—bills, investments, inheritance
4. Health—sickness, disease, depression
5. Marriage—husband, wife, single
6. Children—parenting, barren, adoption
7. Affliction— hardship, torment, sorrow

It's All Good

"And after you have suffered a little while, the God of all grace, who has called you to his eternal glory in Christ, will himself restore, confirm, strengthen, and establish you." (1 Pet. 5:10)

"My child, never forget the things I have taught you. Store my commandments, for length of days and years of life and peace they will add to you. Never let loyalty and kindness leave you! Tie them around your neck as a reminder. Write them deep within your heart. Then you will find favor with both God and people, and you will earn a good reputation. Trust in the Lord with all your heart; do not depend on your own understanding. Seek his will in all you do, and he will show you which path to take." (Prov.3:1–6)

Parenting At Its Best

"For the Lord disciplines the one He loves, just as a father, the son he delights in." (Prov. 3:12).

"Jesus said, "Take my yoke upon you, Let me teach you, because I am humble and gentle at heart, and you will find rest for your souls." (Matt. 11:29)

"Our God is merciful, kind, and loving. He came so that we might have life, and have life more abundantly." (John 10:10).

We may face hardships and challenges within the seven areas of affliction in this world, but take heart, Jesus Christ has overcome the world! When we face it and embrace it; just remember: Jesus Christ' blood has erased it! Be encouraged.

Galatians 2:20

Scripture: "I have been crucified with Christ and I no longer live, but Christ lives in me. The life I now live in the body, I live by faith in the Son of God, who loved me and gave himself for me."

1 Peter 4:12–13

Scripture: "Dear friends, do not be surprised at the fiery ordeal that has come on you to test you, as though something strange were happening to you. But rejoice inasmuch as you participate in the sufferings of Christ, so that you may be overjoyed when his glory is revealed."

> "I rest in the fact that God has chosen me to bless me."
>
> —Bishop TD Jakes

Lesson IV

Kingdom Privilege

"They shall speak of the glory of thy kingdom; and talk of thy power; to make known to the sons of men his mighty acts, and the glorious majesty of his kingdom. Thy kingdom is an everlasting kingdom, and thy dominion endures throughout all generations." (Ps. 145:11–13)

(Jehovah-Hamelech) The King

Introduction:

When Adam and Eve sinned in the Garden of Eden, all of God's children from generation to generation were separated from the Father, so God sent His only begotten Son as the ultimate sacrifice. Jesus Christ the Messiah shed His blood and redeemed us back to the Father, and covered the sins for all of mankind. All was lost. We were enemies to God. We had no way of being reconciled with the Father. The Lord sent His Son Jesus from heaven for us, His children, His beloved, His creation, the apple of His eye.

Objective:

"For our sake he made him to be sin who knew no sin, so that in him we might become the righteousness of God" (2 Cor. 5:21). *(Jehovah- Tsidkenu) The Lord Our Righteousness*

Mission:

"But we are citizens of heaven where the Lord Jesus Christ lives, and we are eagerly waiting for Him to return as our Savior. He will take our weak mortal bodies and change them into glorious bodies like his own, using the same power with which he will bring everything under his control," (Phil. 3:20).

A New Covenant

"Therefore if anyone is in Christ, he is a new creation. The old has passed away. Behold, the new has come! All this is from God, who reconciled us to Himself through Christ and gave us the ministry of reconciliation." (2 Cor. 5:17–18)
"But you are a chosen generation, a royal priesthood, a holy nation, His own special people, that may proclaim the praises of Him who

called you out of darkness into His marvelous light." (1 Pet. 2:9)

The Endless Love of God

Beloved, in addition to our redemption in Jesus Christ, "he does not treat us as our sins deserve or repay us according to our iniquities. For as high as the heavens are above the earth, so great is his love for those who fear him; as far as the east is from the west, so far he removed our transgressions from us" (Rom. 103:10–12). God keeps no records of our wrongs. The Father has seated Jesus on the *"right side"* of the throne of heaven so that you and I will always be in *"right standing"* with Him by the sacrificial blood.

> We are the *"righteousness of God* in Christ Jesus."
>
> —Creflo Dollar

Scripture: "But from now on, the Son of Man will be seated at the right hand of the power of God" (Luke 22:69).

And the Father's grace gives us the opportunity to start each and every day with a clean slate!

"The faithful love of God never ends! His mercies never cease. Great is his faithfulness; his mercies begin afresh each morning" (Lam. 3:22–23).

The Kingdom of God

"For God is the King of all the earth sing to him a psalm of praise. God reigns over the nations; God is seated on his holy throne" (Ps. 47:7–8).

The kingdom of God is the holy of holies, the throne of God, the mercy seat of grace, governing a body of nations in Christ Jesus. It's where the saved children of God possess citizenship and can go boldly to the throne of grace and ask what you will (Heb. 4:16). The kingdom of God is like a dynasty, and the children of God are ambassadors on assignment; and our purpose is to be winners of souls for the kingdom, bringing heaven down to earth through our worship, service, and good deeds.

Proverbs 11:30

Scripture: "The fruit of the righteous is a tree of life; and He that is wise winneth souls."

Matthew 6:10

Scripture: "Thy Kingdom come thy will be done on earth as it is in heaven."

Kingdom Privilege

We have all rights to go before the throne of God and present ourselves as a living sacrifice, holy, acceptable to the Lord; it is our reasonable service (Rom. 12:1.) This verse demonstrates the grace and mercy of God. God instructs us to present ourselves as a living sacrifice, which means we must go to Him in Jesus' name because Jesus is the sacrificial Lamb who shed His blood, and He is holy because He never sinned. When we stand before God in prayer, which is our reasonable service, we stand before God presenting Jesus who is the way, the truth, and the light for mankind. Jesus gives us direct access to God, and the Blood makes us transparent before the Lord.

"Therefore, we go boldly," in Jesus' name, "to the throne of grace that we will obtain and find grace to help in time of need" (Heb. 4:16).

Kingdom Knowledge

In the book of Matthew 18, Jesus explains that "unless we are converted, and become as little children, we shall not enter into the kingdom heaven."

Statistically, it has been proven that children learn faster than adults because the prefrontal cortex of the brain, where working memory is stored, is more developed more in adults than children. Due to the development of the prefrontal cortex, adults experience functional fixedness and that makes adults see everything exactly as it is. However, we cannot enter the kingdom of God seeing through our natural "adult" eyes and/or perceptions. We must first get wisdom, which is the Word of God. Jesus is telling us to dump out the natural way we see, learn, and perceive things. When we go before Him, come with a renewed mind, like the mind of a "child," fully capable, equipped, and willing to absorb His Word; so we will not see things fixated from a carnal "adult" perspective. We will enter His kingdom humble so He can fill us with His wisdom.

Kingdom Inheritance

➢ adoption back into the Kingdom of God;
➢ the Word of God as our bread of life;
➢ direct access to the Father by the Blood of Jesus Christ the Messiah;
➢ the Holy Ghost to lead us, guide us, and intercede for us;
➢ angels assigned to protect us;
➢ dominion and authority over our enemies.

Colossians 1:12–13

Scripture: "Giving thanks to the Father, who has qualified us to share in the inheritance of the saints in Light. For He rescued us from the domain of darkness, and transferred us to the kingdom of his beloved Son."

Lesson V

Wisdom Works

"Do not forsake wisdom, and she will protect
you; love her, and she will watch over you.
The beginning of wisdom is this: Get wisdom. Though
it cost all you have, get understanding." (Prov. 4:6–7)

(Yahweh) The All-Knowing God

Introduction:

During the seventeenth century, the curriculum in the common elementary schools of the New England colonies was summed up as the Four Rs—Reading, 'Riting, 'Rithmetic, and Religion. However in 1825, a member of the parliament, by the name of Sir William Curtis, coined the term *The Three Rs* (as in the letter *R*), which refers to the foundations of *basic, skills*-oriented education program in schools: *reading, writing* and *arithmetic.*

Since its original creation, the term is used to describe other trifecta. *The Three Rs* is a widely used abbreviation for the basic elements of a primary school curriculum—reading, 'riting (writing), and 'rithmetic (arithmetic). *The Three Rs* trifecta is still utilized today in the twenty-first century within the education curriculum. Another *The Three Rs* common trifecta implemented today is (reading, 'riting (writing), and *reciting.* The goal and objective of *read, write,* and *recite* is to instruct students through multiple-intelligence sensory stimulants. Reading is seeing it, writing is the tactile stimulus, and reciting is for auditory stimulation.

Objective:

"Blessed are those who find wisdom, those who gain understanding" (Prov. 3:13).

Mission:

"If any of you lacks wisdom, you should ask God, who gives generously to all without finding fault, and it will be given to you" (James 1:5).

Reading with a Purpose

Once the human eyes fall on a word, a complex set of processes—physical, neurological, and cognitive abilities—is set in motion, enabling us to convert print into meaning. Nerve impulses from the eyes stimulate an area near the back of the brain that allows us to see the light and dark areas on a page that define each letter. Behind the frontal lobe on the right side of the brain, in the posterior (back part), is called the parietal lode.

This area is responsible for reading, writing, and arithmetic and the brain further forward allows us to convert the letters we see into sounds and those sounds into language. Finally, the brain converts the jumble of words in any given sentence into something meaningful that we can interpret. The four components of reading and learning to read is a continuous process; each new skill builds on the mastery of previously learned skills.

Each step in the process relates to one of the three components of reading: decoding, comprehension, or retention. These are the component tasks of reading and also in a general view, the progressive steps in learning to read, which move from sounds, to words, to sentences, and paragraphs.

> "He read it aloud from daybreak till noon as he faced the square before the Water Gate in the presence of the men, women and others who could understand. And all the people listened attentively to the Book of the Law." (Neh. 8:3)

Writing with a Purpose

Writing is to express oneself, to provide information, to persuade, or to create a literary work. There are four purposes writers use for writing. When someone communicates ideas in writing, they usually do so to express themselves, inform their reader, to persuade a reader, or to create a literary work. This is what the LORD, the God of Israel, says, "Write in a book all the words I have spoken to you" (Jer. 30:2).

Reciting is the Purpose

Saying words out loud are remembered much better than those that are read silently. The words we speak aloud are translated into speech, and we obtain more knowledge that is effective to the memory. If we hear or speak words out loud, the information that is spoken increases our motor memory skills and is distinctly different from words that are read silently.

"Faith comes by hearing and hearing by the Word of God" (Rom. 10:17).

How We Retain Information

10 percent of what we read,
20 percent of what we hear,
30 percent of what we see,
50 percent of what we hear and see,
70 percent of what we say, and
90 percent of what we say and do.

Faith without works is dead, (James 2).

Scripture:

"And it shall come to pass, if thou shalt hearken diligently unto the voice of the Lord thy God, to observe and do all his commandments which I command thee this day, that the Lord thy God will set thee on high above all the nations on the earth. And all these blessing shall come on thee, and over take thee, if thou shalt hearken unto the voice of the Lord thy God." (Deut. 28:1–2)

It's Your Call

Scripture: "Blessed are those who find wisdom, those who gain understanding" (Prov. 3:13).

The Lord teaches us in scripture to first, "get wisdom and understanding" (Prov. 4:6–7). Activating *The Three Rs,* "read, 'rite (write), and recite trifecta from a biblical principle, or perspective, puts us in agreement with the Word of God, creating prosperity and purpose for our lives.

- *Read* the Word of God—"Renew the mind, mediate on the word day and night, and then you shall make your way prosperous" (Josh. 1:8).
- *Write* down a plan—"Write it on a tablet, make it simple" (Hab. 2:3).
- *Recite* the Word of God—"Confession is made unto salvation" (Rom. 10:10).

Psalm 19:2

Scripture: "Day after day they pour forth speech; night after night they reveal knowledge."

Proverb 29:18

Scripture: "Without a vision, the people perish."

Proverbs 18:15

Scripture: "The heart of the discerning acquires knowledge, for the ears of the wise seek it out."

"The Secret Of Your Future Is Hidden In Your Dailey Routine."

—Mike Murdock

It All Begins with Structure

God is a God of order, principles, timing, and seasons. We must practice the principles and instructions of God through His Word. God introduced the Word first, before Himself. Scripture tells us that "the Word became life and dwelt among us" (John 1:14). Jesus is the walking and talking Word full of grace and truth. "For the Word of God is alive and active. Sharper than any double-edged sword, it penetrates even to dividing soul and spirit, joints and marrow; it judges the thoughts and attitudes of the heart" (Heb. 4:12). Mediating on the Word of God builds faith and hope, and it binds fear and frustration.

Scripture: "If you abide in me, and my Words abide in you, ask whatever you wish, and it will be done for you" (John 15:7).

Lesson VI

The Holy Spirit

"Then the angel showed me the river of the water of life, as clear as crystal, flowing from the throne of God and of the Lamb down the middle of the great street of the city. On each side of the river stood the tree of life, bearing twelve crops of fruit, yielding its fruit every month. And the leaves of the tree are for the healing of the nations." (Rev. 22:1–2)

(Yeshua - Hamashiach) The Anointed One

Introduction:

Genesis 1:1–10 says, "In the beginning God created the heavens and the earth. Now the earth was formless and empty, darkness was over the surface of the deep, and the Spirit of God was hovering over the waters. And God said, 'Let there be light,' and there was light. God saw that the light was good, and he separated the light from the darkness. God called the light 'day,' and the darkness he called 'night.' And there was evening, and there was morning—the first day. And God said, 'Let there be a vault between the waters to separate water from water.' So God made the vault and separated the water under the vault from the water above it. And it was so. God called the vault 'sky.' And there was evening, and there was morning—the second day. And God said, 'Let the water under the sky be gathered to one place, and let dry ground appear.' And it was so. God called the dry ground 'land,' and the gathered waters he called 'seas.' And God saw that it was good."

As God continued to create land, galaxy, living creatures, and the body and soul of mankind (Gen. 1:11–31), we only read about the Spirit of God moving once while hovering over the face of the waters. And whenever the Spirit of God moves or dwells, it anoints. God anointed the waters and then he began to create everything on earth from the waters by His Word and His Spirit.

Objective:

"The Spirit itself beareth witness with our spirit, that we are the children of God" (Rom. 8:16).

Mission:

"Being filled with power is the Spirit of the Lord" (Mic. 3:8).

It's in the Water

Water is vital for life on earth. Where there is no water, there is no life; and where there is scarcity of water, life has to struggle. The earth's surface is covered by 70 percent of water and water also exists in the air as water vapor, in rivers and lakes, in icecaps and glaciers, in the ground as soil moisture and in aquifers, and even animals. The human body is made up of 70 percent water, and staying hydrated is so very important. The body needs water to maintain the balance of body fluids. Maintenance of body temperature, digestion and absorption of food, and circulation of blood, these are all functions the body will be unable to perform if it doesn't get enough water.

Jesus' parable teachings in the gospels illustrates Him as being the anointed water that will never run dry for mankind. He spoke knowledge and wisdom to the Samaritan women at the well, enlightening her "that if she drank of his water she would never thirst again" (John 4:10).

In John chapter 7, Jesus said, "Whoever believes in him rivers of living water will flow from their heart."

Mankind and Water

Water is a colorless, transparent, tasteless liquid that forms the seas, lake, rivers, and rain, and is the basis of the fluids of living organisms that helps get rid of toxins. Without water, the body wouldn't be able to get rid of toxins that can cause damage to cells and organ. Water keeps the digestive system flowing, and when there is an adequate amount of water flowing in the body, the digestive system is able to process at a normal flow. However, if there is a lack of water, the colon will begin to pull from the stools to get enough water to digest. The right amount of water intake for the body ensures healthier looking eyes and skin. A 1-percent deficiency of the normal body water percentage can cause fatigue and 2–4 percent can affect mental functioning. Drinking water helps weight loss and can prevent heart disease.

Water Bearing Witness: The Baptism

Before Jesus started His ministry, He first was baptized in the Jordan River. God speaks and introduces His Son Jesus during His baptism, and the Holy Spirit descends from heaven like a dove. Here we see, like in Genesis, the Spirit of God hovering over the waters but this time, to anoint Jesus.

"Go ye therefore, and make disciples of all the nations, baptizing them into the name of the Father and of the Son and of the Holy Ghost" (Matt. 28:19).

The Ark

When God decided to destroy the world, He instructed Noah to build the Ark. The earth was fully covered once again with water. God bought everything He had created on earth outside of the Ark back to Himself by His Spirit, and with the waters, he cleansed the earth.

Humanity

God's Word and Spirit are vital, like water for our bodies. The human body cannot live or function without water. The Holy Spirit is the anointing that overflows like water. Jesus prayed for man in 3 John, Beloved: "I pray that in all respects you may prospers and be in good health, just as your souls prospers." Our bodies require water, and our souls thirst for the Word; the Spirit man feeds off the Word and anoints us to do greater works.

It's Heartfelt

The Holy Ghost dwells inside of our hearts; but in order for the Body, Soul, and the Spirit man to be healthy, it requires the Word of God, which is food for man. Jesus answered, "Man shall not live by bread alone but by every Word that proceeds out of the mouth of God" (Matt. 4:4). When we begin to feed our minds with the Word of God, the anointing of God, the Holy Spirit will begin to pour out of our hearts and overflow like rivers of living water.

2 Corinthians 1:21–22

Scripture: "Now it is God who makes both us and you stand firm in Christ. He anointed us, set his seal of ownership on us, and put his Spirit in our hearts as a deposit, guaranteeing what is to come."

1 John 2:27

Scripture: "As for you, the anointing you received from him remains in you, and you do not need anyone to teach you. But as his anointing teaches you about all things and as that anointing is real, not counterfeit, just as it has taught you, remain in him."

1 Corinthians 6:19

Scripture: "Do you not know that your body is a temple of the Holy Spirit, who is in you, whom you have received from God?"

1 John 4:4

Scripture: "He that dwells within is greater than he that is in the world."

The Oil Anointing

The blessing of oil symbolizes the Holy Spirit who leads us into all truths and "anoints" us continually with His power, grace, and comfort. Oil anointing is a scared act of faith and worship to be set apart and dedicated to serving God. It's symbolic to the blessings and gifts, consecration, prayer, healing, and worship to be divinely designated, inaugurated, or chosen for some purpose by God. The word *anoint* appears in more than 150 Spirit-inspired scriptures in various contextual forms. The English word *anoint* derives from the ancient Latin "*inunctus*" meaning, "smear of oil." In John 12:3, we see Mary anointing the feet of Jesus with oil as an act of worship before His crucifixion.

Anointed for a Purpose

- ➢ Jesus' feet washed with tears and oil (Luke 7:38)
- ➢ Healing of sickness and disease (Exod. 29:7, James 5:14–16)
- ➢ Cast out demons (Mark 6:13)
- ➢ Ruth anoints herself to meet with Boaz (Ruth 3:3)
- ➢ Minister to others (Isaiah 61:1)
- ➢ Consecration (Lev. 8:30, Lev. 8:12, Exod. 30:30, Exod. 40:9, and Ps. 23)
- ➢ Matrimonial (Exod. 25:6)
- ➢ Generational blessing (Exod. 30:31)
- ➢ Samuel anoints David to be king (1 Sam. 16:13)
- ➢ Fasting (Dan. 10:3 and Matt. 6:17)
- ➢ Burial preparation (Mark 14:8)
- ➢ War (Isa. 21:5)
- ➢ Breaking of yokes (Isa. 21:5)
- ➢ Worship (Mark 14:3–9)
- ➢ Strength (Isa. 61:3)
- ➢ Holiness (Exod. 30:25)
- ➢ Communion (Exod. 30:26–29)
- ➢ Jacob sets up a memorial (Gen. 28:18)

Scripture: "God anoints Jesus with the oil of gladness, after He triumphantly returns to heaven" (Heb. 1:9).

Midterm Exam

"But the Helper, the Holy Spirit, whom the Father will send in My name, He will teach you all things, and bring to your remembrance all I said to you."(John 14:26)

(Yahweh) I Am

Midterm Exam

1. The Father described the creation, purpose, and plan of mankind to whom?

2. God created mankind, and the covenant had six things about the past and future of man. What were the six things?

3. The depths of our relationship with the Father are so intricate that He knows us individually by what?

4. Did we have an intimate relationship with the Father before he formed us in the womb?
   TRUE   FALSE

5. What is God saying in Acts 17:26, "And He made from one man every nation to live on all the face of the earth, having determined their appointed times and the boundaries of their habitation"?

6. Who is Jesus the light and life of?

7. Who is the Trinity?

8. What are the three parts of man functioning as one?

9. We are not made in the image of God.
   TRUE   FALSE

10. The "body" of mankind functions from what?

11. Name mankind's soul attributes?

12. What is the purpose of mankind's spirit?
    A. Faith   B. Hope
    C. Reverence   D. Prayer
    E. Worship   F. All of the above

13. Did Jesus Christ redeem all of mankind out of all of our sins by His precious Blood?
    TRUE   FALSE

14. How can one become saved?
    A. Recite the sinner's prayer   B. Believe with all of your heart
    C. Believe with all of your   D. Believe with all of your soul
       mind
    E. Confess that Jesus Christ   F. All of the above
       is your Savior and
       Redeemer, and that He
       died and rose again.

15. Name the seven reasons why Jesus Christ shed His blood for mankind?

16. There are nine Gifts of the Spirit; which group is not a gift?
    A. Wisdom and knowledge   B. Faith and healing
    C. Miraculous powers   D. Fear and anxiousness
    E. Prophecy and distinguish F. Speaking in tongues and
       between Spirits   tongue interpretation

17. Are the seven mountains of purpose: religion, family, education, government media, arts, and entertainment?
    TRUE   FALSE

18. Name the seven areas that we may encounter test, trials, and tribulation in our lives?

19. What is Jesus professing in John 16:33 when he says, "I have told you these things, so that in me you may have peace. In this world, you will have trouble. But take heart! I have overcome the world!"

20. What are the nine Fruits of the Spirit?

21. If we are in Christ, we are a new creation, and there is no condemnation.
TRUE   FALSE

22. Why did the Father sit Jesus at His right-hand side in heaven?

23. Is it doctrine that we are in the world but not from this world?
TRUE   FALSE

24. Where do the children of God possess citizenship?

25. God keeps no record of mankind's wrongs.
TRUE   FALSE

26. We are ambassadors for the kingdom of God.
TRUE   FALSE

27. How do we get direct access to the throne of God?
A. God's unconditional Love   B. The Blood of Jesus
C. God's grace and mercy   D. All of the above

28. What are The Three Rs' practices when it comes to getting wisdom?

29. Does God inform us to get "wisdom" first to be prosperous?
TRUE   FALSE

30. Which part of the Trinity is the anointing of God Almighty?

31. In what area of mankind's body does the Holy Ghost dwell?

32. What is the Holy Spirit's sole purpose for mankind?
    A. Intercession   B. Guidance
    C. Teaching   D. Anointing
    E. Advocating   F. All of the above

33. What is mankind's purpose?
    A. Win souls for the   B. Feed the hungry and
       kingdom of God   clothe the poor
    C. Be a blessing to others D. Pray for one another
    E. Spread the good news F. All of the above

34. What does the name *Yeshua Hamashiach* mean?

35. Does scripture say we should be baptized in the name of the
    Father, Son, and Holy Ghost?
    TRUE   FALSE

36. Heaven opened up, the Father spoke, and the Holy Spirit
    descended like a dove to anoint Jesus. What was Jesus doing?

37. Has God anointed you with Gifts of the Spirit to be purpose-
    ful on earth?
    TRUE   FALSE

Midterm Exam Answer Key

1. The Father described the creation, purpose, and plan of man-kind to whom?

   Jeremiah

2. God created mankind, and the covenant had six things about the past and future of man. What were the six things?

   Identity, Relationship, Formation, Consecration, Purpose, Assignment

3. The depths of our relationship with the Father are so intricate that He knows us individually by what?

   By every individual hair strand on our heads

4. Did we have an intimate relationship with the Father before He formed us in the womb?

   TRUE   FALSE

5. What is God saying in Acts: 17:26, "And He made from one man every nation to live on all the face of the earth, having determined their appointed times and the boundaries of their habitation"?

   We are one nation under God created by one man, ordained to fulfill our purpose at the appointed season.

6. Who is Jesus the light and life of?
   Mankind

7. Who is the Trinity?
   Father, Son, Holy Ghost

8. What are the three parts of man functioning as one?
   Body, Soul, Spirit

9. We are not made in the image of God.
   TRUE   **FALSE**

10. The "body" of mankind functions from what?
    Five senses

11. Name mankind's Soul attributes.
    Imagination, Conscious, Memory, Reasoning, and Affection

12. What is the purpose of mankind's Spirit?
    A. Faith   B. Hope
    C. Reverence   D. Prayer
    E. Worship   ***F. All of the above***

13. Did Jesus Christ redeem all of mankind out of all of our sins
    by His precious blood?
    TRUE   FALSE

14. How can one become saved?
    A. Recite the sinner's prayer   B. Believe with all
                                        of your heart

    C. Believe with all of your   D. Believe with all of your soul
    mind

E. Confess that Jesus Christ is your Savior and Redeemer and that He died and rose again.

F. *All of the above*

15. Name the seven reasons why Jesus Christ shed His blood for mankind?

    For mankind to possess Freedom, Healing, Prosperity, Dominion, Authority, Peace, and Restoration

16. There are nine Gifts of the Spirit. Which group is not a gift?

    A. Wisdom and knowledge
    B. Faith and healing
    C. Miraculous powers
    D. *Fear and anxiousness*
    E. Prophecy and distinguish between Spirits
    F. Speaking in tongues and tongue interpretation

17. Are the seven mountains of purpose: religion, family, education, government media, arts, and entertainment?
    TRUE   FALSE

18. Name the seven areas that we may encounter test, trials, and tribulation in our lives?

    Family, Work, Finances, Health, Marriage, Children, and Business

19. What is Jesus professing in John 16:33 when he says, "I have told you these things, so that in me you may have peace. In this world you will have trouble. But take heart! I have overcome the world!"

    To fear not because every issue we may encounter, we will overcome it and be victorious like Him.

20. What are the nine Fruits of the Spirit?

Love, Joy, Peace, Longsuffering, Kindness, Goodness, Faithfulness, Gentleness and Self-Control

21. If we are in Christ, we are a new creation, and there is no condemnation.
TRUE   FALSE

22. Why did the Father sit Jesus at His right-hand side in heaven?

Because Jesus has redeemed us to be in right standing with the Father through His blood sacrifice, and now we are the righteousness of God in Christ Jesus.

23. Is it doctrine that we are in the world but not from this world?
TRUE   FALSE

24. Where do the children of God possess citizenship?

In the kingdom of heaven

25. God keeps no record of mankind's wrongs.
TRUE   FALSE

26. We are ambassadors for the kingdom of God?
TRUE   FALSE

27. How do we get direct access to the throne of God?

A. God's unconditional Love B. The Blood of Jesus

C. God's grace and mercy   ***D. All of the above***

28. What are The Three R's practices when it comes to getting wisdom?

Reading, Writing, and Reciting God's Word produces wisdom

29. Does God inform us to get "wisdom" first to be prosperous?
TRUE   FALSE

30. Which part of the Trinity is the anointing of God almighty?
The Holy Spirit

31. In what area of mankind's body does the Holy Ghost dwell?
Our hearts

32. What is the Holy Spirit's sole purpose for mankind?
A. Intercession   B. Guidance
C. Teaching   D. Anointing
E. Advocating   **F. All of the above**

33. What is mankind's purpose?
A. Win souls for the king- B. Feed the hungry and clothe
dom of God   the poor
C. Be a blessing to others D. Pray for one another
E. Spread the good news   **F. All of the above**

34. What does the name *Yeshua Hamashiach* mean?
The Anointed One

35. Does scripture say we should be baptized in the name of the Father, Son, and Holy Ghost?
TRUE   FALSE

36. Heaven opened up, the Father spoke, and the Holy Spirit descended like a dove to anoint Jesus; what was Jesus doing?
Jesus was being baptized.

37. Has God anointed you with Gifts of the Spirit to be purposeful on earth?
TRUE   FALSE

Lesson VII

The Principles of God Part 1

"Please receive instruction from his mouth and establish his words in your heart." (Job 22:22)

(El Echad) The One God

Introduction:

First, go to God with everything in prayer: ourselves, health, marriage, children, career, finances, family, friends, uncertainties, fears, confusion, wisdom, discussions, commitments, disagreements, struggles, anxieties, depression, and addictions. God said, "Draw near to Him, and He will draw near to us" (James 4:8).

When we commit our ways to the Lord, through Christ, we access our rights in the kingdom of God. The book of Psalms tells us, "The steps of a good man are ordered by the Lord: and he delighteth in his way." The Father knows what is best for us. He is our creator; trust in Him. "He will never leave you nor forsake you" (Deut. 31:8).

We need to put all of our faith in the Lord. God's way is the only way. "I will bless the Lord who has counseled me; indeed my mind instructs me in the night. I have set the LORD continually before me; Because He is at my right hand, I will not be shaken" (Ps.16:7–8).

Objective:

"Seek yea first the kingdom of God and his righteousness, and all these things shall be added onto you," (Matt 6:33)
(El - Elyon) God Most High

Mission:

"He is on the path of life who heeds instruction, but he who forsakes reproof goes astray." (Prov. 10:17)

There are principles and instructions in the kingdom of God; and in order to become fruitful in every area of our lives, we need to implement and practice the principles of God. "Order my steps in your word; and let not any iniquity have dominion over me" (Ps. 119:133).

The First Fruits Principle

First, acknowledge God with your time every morning when you rise, before the start of the day, with praise, worship, and thanksgiving.

First, go to God in prayer about all things. "Everything to the Lord in prayer."

First, give God 10 percent of all of our earnings, and God said, "He will rebuke the devourer" from robbing, killing, and destroying the remaining 90 percent of our income. The tithe is like a business proposal; it's an investment. Tithing is the only area in the Bible where God says to "try Him and see what the results will be." If we give or "invest" 10 percent of our earnings faithfully, He will open up the windows of heaven and pour out blessings that there will not be enough room for us to contain, the overflow return of the blessings. Malachi 3:10 is a lucrative financial investment for the citizens of the kingdom of God.

"The plans of the diligent lead surely to advantage, but everyone who is hasty comes surely to poverty." (Prov. 21:5)

Isaiah 48:17

Scripture: "Thus says the Lord, your Redeemer, the Holy One of Israel: I am the Lord your God, who teachers you to profit, who leads you in the way you should go."

Deuteronomy 8:18

Scripture: "But remember the Lord your God, for it is he who gives you the ability to produce wealth, and so confirms his covenant, which he swore to your ancestors, as it is today."

> "The problem is not the lack of money;
> it's the lack of revelation."
> —Paula White

Faith Principle

Faith is complete trust or confidence in someone or something, strong belief in God or in the doctrines of religion based on spiritual apprehension rather than proof.

The Doctrines of Faith

Faith comes by hearing the Word of God. (Rom. 10:17)
Faith sets its heart on the principles of God. (Heb. 6:1)
Faith brings joy and peace. (Rom. 5:1)
Faith heals. (Ps. 107:19–20)
Faith brings the glory of God. (John 11:40)
Faith saves. (Eph. 2:8)
Righteous will live by faith. (Hab. 2:4)
Faith makes us whole. (Luke 17–19)
Faith brings confidence. (Hebrew 11:1)
Faith shields us with God's power. (1 Pet. 1:5)
Faith forgives. (Matt. 9:2)
Faith establishes love. (Eph. 3:16–17)

"And without faith, it is impossible to please God." (Heb. 11:6)

The Meditation Principle

Here, we see The Three Rs applied.
Meditation—the act of meditation, contemplation, and reflection. "Meditate on the Word, day and night, then you will make your way prosperous" (Josh. 1:8).

> ➢ **Read** the Word of God, study. We know that reading is fundamental, then we must also know that reading and meditating on the Word of God is essential as well. "Study to show thyself approved unto God," (2 Tim. 2:15).

Supplication Principle

A petition is a written document. A request made for something desired, especially a respectful or humble request as to a superior or to one of those in authority; a supplication or prayer. "Be anxious for nothing, but in everything, by prayer *supplication* and thanksgiving, let your request be made known to God," (Phil. 4:6).

> ➤ *Write.* Keep a journal of scriptures, thoughts, and ideas. When the Holy Ghost speaks to us, guides, and directs us, we should write it down, include times and dates. Writing stimulates the visual senses; it promotes mental learning when we see it on paper. "Write it down on a tablet make it plain" (Hab. 2:3).

Confession Principle

> ➤ *Recite.* Confess and decree victory over situations, circumstances, and trials through the Word of God out loud. It's crucial that we hear ourselves. Repetition and reinforcement stimulates the cognitive process. Establish a daily routine in the Word; command things to come and go, "recollect." We have the authority to do so by the shedding of Jesus Christ's blood. "I have declared my ways. Open confession is good for the soul" (Ps. 119:26).

Thanksgiving Principle

Thanksgiving is the expression of gratitude especially to God. "In everything, give thanks; for this is the will of God in Christ Jesus for you" (1 Thess. 5:18). God expresses to us that we ought to be thankful to Him because of His unconditional love, grace, mercy, generosity, knowledge, wisdom, creation, righteousness, strength, faithfulness, goodness, greatness, joyfulness, peace, hopefulness, and good judgment.

The Father, "says to be thankful through psalms, hymns, and songs from the Spirit, singing to God with gratitude in our hearts. And whatever you do, whether in word or deed, do it all in the name of the Lord Jesus, giving thanks to God the Father through him" (Col. 3:16–17).

Being thankful to the Lord demonstrates gratitude, which in return is "all for your benefit so that grace that is reaching more and more people may cause thanksgiving to overflow to the glory of God" (2 Cor. 4:15).

Seedtime and Harvest Principle

Giving connects us to the seedtime and harvest principle. When we give, it's different from the tithe because Yeshua specifically instructs us on how much to give, which is ten percent of all of our earnings. But the seedtime principle is what we give or sow from our hearts. God has given us the opportunity to sow a seed toward our needs. The Word tells us the seeds we sow will produce a harvest during the appointed season for our lives or in the lives of others that we stand in the gap and intercede for, these seeds are biblically known as "sustainment seeds." God will sustain us through trials, tribulations, and unforeseen situations. The seedtime and harvest principle will reverse a curse, bring healing, provide a financial breakthrough, and cover us protecting our present and future. The Bible says, "Whatever a man sows, that he will also reap" (Gal. 6:7). "Give and it shall be given to you. A good measure, pressed down, shaken together, and running over, will be poured into your lap. For with the measure you use, it will be measured to you" (Luke 6:38). The earth remains, Seedtime and harvest, Cold and heat, Winter and summer, And day and night shall not cease" (Gen. 8:22).

"Always sow a seed toward your need."
—Oral Roberts and Rod Parsley

Agreement Principle

"If two of you shall agree on earth as touching anything that they shall ask, it shall be done for them by my father which is in heaven." (Matt. 18:19)

"One will put one thousand to flight, but two will put ten thousand to flight." (Lev.26:8, Deut. 32:30)

Vision Principle

Vision (noun)—an experience of seeing someone or something in a dream or trance or as a supernatural apparition.

Vision (verb)—imagine; a mental image of what the future will or could be.

"Where there is no vision the people perish" (Prov. 29:18). Get a picture, draw a picture or create a vision board; because what we see, is what we get.

Visions from Head Start

In preschool drawing comes before writing. Children draw shapes and illustrations, then they attach syntax to it. Drawing is one of the early foundations of abstract thought or logical thinking. It aids in the development of a child's problem-solving skills; boosts confidence; and enhances motor skills, concentration, imagination, and creativity. It makes school ready, brings joy, promotes intrinsic motivation, and sharpens almost all cognitive processes that a child needs to sharpen their mind.

This is why God says, "Without a vision, we will perish." First, get a mental image or vision. Obtain both a mental picture and physical one. What should we do to keep the vision alive? I'm glad you asked. Read a scripture that correlates to the situation. Write down what you expect the outcome to be in alignment with God's Word. "Petition," make it plain. Confess it; it will come to pass. "It will not tarry; it will not delay." If we expect it to come to pass, it will in due season because it's already done in heaven.

Baptism Principle

Baptism is an important event in the believer's walk with Jesus Christ. The Bible talks about both water immersion baptisms in which a believer makes a public confession of their faith. Jesus was publicly baptized, and the Father was very proud. Scripture tells us that when all the people were being baptized, Jesus was baptized too. And as He was praying, the heavens were opened, and the Holy Spirit descended on Him in bodily form like a dove. And a voice came from heaven: "You are my Son, whom I love; with you I am well pleased" (Luke 3:21–22).

Mark 16:16
Scripture: "Whoever believes and is baptized will be saved, but whoever does not believe will be condemned."

One Baptism, One Spirit

"For we were all baptized by one Spirit so as to form one body, whether Jews or Gentiles, slave or free, and we were all given the one Spirit to drink." (1 Cor. 12:13)

Acts 2:38
Scripture: "Then Peter said unto them, Repent, and be baptized every one of you in the name of Jesus Christ for the forgiveness of sins, and you will receive the gift of the Holy Spirit."

The Wait is Over

"And now what are you waiting for? Get up, be baptized and wash your sins away, calling on his name." (Acts 22:16)

Fasting Principle

Fast—to abstain from all or some kinds of food or drink, especially as a religious observance.

First, determine why you are you fasting. Is it for spiritual renewal, for guidance, for healing, for the resolution of problems, for special grace to handle a difficult situation? Ask the Holy Spirit to clarify His leading and objectives for your prayer fast. This will enable you to pray more specifically and strategically.

Make a Commitment

- How long you will fast—one meal, one day, a week, several weeks, forty days (Beginners should start slowly, building up to longer fasts.)
- The type of fast God wants you to undertake (such as water only, or water and juices; what kinds of juices you will drink and how often)
- What physical or social activities you will restrict.
- How much time each day you will devote to prayer and God's Word.

Prepare Spiritually

- Ask God to help you make a comprehensive list of your sins.
- Confess every sin that the Holy Spirit calls to your remembrance and accept God's forgiveness. (1 John 1:9)
- Seek forgiveness from all whom you have offended, and forgive all who have hurt you. (Mark 11:25; Luke 11:4; 17:3–4)
- Make restitution as the Holy Spirit leads you.
- Ask God to fill you with His Holy Spirit according to His command in Ephesians 5:18 and His promise in 1 John 5:14–15.

- Surrender your life fully to Jesus Christ as your Lord and Master; refuse to obey your worldly nature. (Rom. 12:1–2)
- Meditate on the attributes of God, His love, sovereignty, power, wisdom, faithfulness, grace, compassion, and others. (Ps. 48:9,10; 103:1–8, 11–13)
- Begin your time of fasting and prayer with an expectant heart. (Heb. 11:6)
- Do not underestimate spiritual opposition. Satan sometimes intensifies the natural battle between body and spirit. (Gal. 5:16–17)

Prepare Yourself Physically

Fasting requires reasonable precautions. Consult your physician first especially if you take prescription medication or have a chronic ailment. Some persons should never fast without professional supervision.

Physical preparation makes the drastic change in your eating routine a little easier so that you can turn your full attention to the Lord in prayer.

- Do not rush into your fast.
- Prepare your body. Eat smaller meals before starting a fast. Avoid high fat and sugary foods.
- Eat raw fruit and vegetables for two days before starting a fast.

Dr. Bill Right

Matthew 6:16–18

Scripture: "When you fast, do not look somber as the hypocrites do, for they disfigure their faces to show others they are fasting. Truly, I tell you, they have received their reward in full. But when you fast, put oil on your head and wash your face, so that it will not be obvious to others that you are fasting, but only to your Father, who is unseen; and your Father, who sees what is done in secret, will reward you."

Communion Principle

Why communion? Communion began on the annual celebration of Passover, when Jesus told His disciples to remember His sacrifice as they ate the bread and drank the wine. So believers in Jesus Christ celebrate and remember His sacrifice of our sins when He died on the cross. Holy Communion uses bread as a symbol of Jesus Christ's body and wine as a symbol of blood He shed. The act of taking communion does not save us; it is an act of worship and remembrance.

"And he took bread, gave thanks and broke it, and gave it to them, saying, 'This is my body given for you; do this in remembrance of me.'" (Acts 27:35)

Luke 22:19–20

Scripture: "In the same way, after the supper, he took the cup, saying, 'This cup is the new covenant in my blood, which is poured out for you.'"

Lesson *VIII*

The Principles of God Part 2

"Then Jesus told his disciples a parable to show them that they should always pray and not give up." (Luke 18:1)

(Jehovah – Kabodhi) The Lord My Glory

Introduction:

Most people refrain from prayer because they are unsure of how to pray. The thought of praying can be intimidating for many believers due to the fear of not using the correct "religious etiquette." Or thinking that the prayer maybe too short, God can't hear them, or they are just not sure of what to address in the prayer. In the Lord's Prayer (Matt. 6:9–13), Jesus gives us a full description on the principles of prayer. There are seven principles within The Lords' Prayer, providing us with guidance and instruction. Jesus is direct and precise from beginning to end.

Objective:

"Pray continually." (1 Thess. 5:17)

Mission:

"May these words of my mouth and this meditation of my heart be pleasing in your sight, LORD, my Rock and my Redeemer." (Ps. 19:14)

The Principles of Prayer

Below, we will dissect the Lord's Prayer and identify how Jesus instructed the disciples on how to pray the effective prayer verse by verse:

"Our Father which art in heaven, hallowed be your name."
1. **(Honor: God is Holy)**

"Thy kingdom come, Thy will be done, on earth as it is in heaven."
2. **(Confession)**

> "Give us this day our daily bread."
> 3. **(Agreement with His Word)**

> "And forgive us *our* debts,"
> 4. **(Repentance)**

> "As we also have forgiven *our* debtors."
> 5. **(Forgiveness)**

> "And lead us not into temptation, but deliver us from evil."
> 6. **(Rebuke the Enemy)**

> "For thine is the kingdom, and the power, and the glory, forever. Amen."
> 7. **(Praise and Worship)**

Prayer Made Simple

Don't fall prey to "wishful thinking" or let your emotions get the best of you. Find out what the Bible says about your situation or circumstances and include it in the prayer.

Create a Personalized Prayer

Materials: pen and journal

Instruction

Choose one or more lines from each prayer principle to create a personalized prayer.

God Has Many Names (see the Names of God)

Choose *one* to begin prayer

- Father
- Yeshua—Jesus
- Elohim—God Creator
- Yahweh—Lord
- El Shaddai—God Almighty
- Jehovah Jireh—Lord, My Provider
- Jehovah Rapha—Lord, My Healer

Honor

Choose one or more.

- Holy, Holy, Holy is thy name
- I give you the highest praise, hallelujah.
- I honor you.
- You are faithful and true.
- You are worthy.
- I thank you.
- I love you.

Confession

Choose one or more.

- God, you are the same yesterday, today, and forevermore.
- Whatsoever I bind and loose on earth shall be bound and loosed in heaven.
- I call those things to be not as though they were.
- In you, Lord, I move, live, and have my being, not my will but thy will be done.
- Father, you are not a man that you should lie.

- Your Word shall never return onto you void.
- Your mercy and grace endures forever.

Agreement

Choose one or more.

- Your Word is a lamp to my feet.
- By your stripes, I am healed.
- If I draw near to you, you will draw near to me.
- Lead me, guide me, order my steps.
- Stir up the gifts in me.
- I am not my own; I belong to you.

Repentance

Choose one or more.

- I repent my sins of _____.
- I confess my sins of _____.
- Search my heart; remove what is not of you.
- Wash me as clean as snow.
- Forgive me of my sins.
- Cleanse me by the Blood.
- Baptize me in the Holy Ghost.

Forgiveness

(Apply all)

- Lord, forgive me for my transgressions. Change me by your mighty power. Teach me to always love. Let your light so shine upon me that others will see more of you and less of me. Teach me to be a blessing to others in my daily walk.

(Apply all or as many as needed)

- I forgive all that have hurt me, betrayed me, deceived me, used me, abused me, cursed me, lied on me, mistreated me, abandoned me, mislead me, cheated on me, stole from me, envious of me, jealous of me and have judged me.

Rebuke the Devil

(Apply one or more)

- No weapon formed against me shall be able to prosper.
- I rebuke the devourer over my life and circumstances.
- I shall not live by bread alone, but I shall live by every Word that proceeds out of the mouth of God.
- Jesus, cover me with your wings and keep me protected in the blood.
- Lord, I put on your whole amour today, shield me with your mighty right hand.
- I resist you, Satan, and your lies. You have no influence or control over me.
- I have dominion and authority over the enemy, and I cast him back into the pits of hell!

Praise and Worship

(Choose one or more)

- Thank you, Yeshua. You are worthy to be praised.
- Great are you, Lord. Your mercy and grace endures forever.
- Jehovah, you are faithful and just, I magnify you.
- Yahweh, I honor you. You are sovereign and the only true God.

- Abba, Father, I exalt your name day and night.
- My God, I give you thanks, with all of my heart. I will sing praises onto your Holy Name.

End Prayer

In Jesus' name. Amen—so be it.

The Principle of Expectation

Expectation is a strong belief that something will happen or be the case in the future. Expectation is hope, and hope is a feeling of expectation and desire for a certain thing to happen. Therefore, we aspire and prepare during the waiting period, and never lose hope. When we put our trust and faith in God, we can "expect" that He will be with us. God loves us all, and He only wants the absolute best for us, which may consist of testing trials. However, we are assured that the trails are ordained to guide us toward our blessings.

Seven Ways to Keep Expectation Alive

Hope—never *stop*!
Ambition—be determined and do your part: apply God's principles.
Aspire—want it enough and don't stop wanting it until it comes to fruition.
Wish—ask God to show you a sign.
Aim—have a clear visual of the target.
Plan —prepare yourself for what's to come.
Desire—make sure the desire is not just in your head. Want it bad enough that it flows from your heart.

"For I know the plans I have for you; plans to prosper you and not harm you, plans to give you hope and a future." (Jer. 29:11)

Principle of Patience

Patience is the capacity to accept or tolerate delay, trouble, or suffering without getting angry or upset.

Waiting on our time or season to manifest can seem difficult, and cause feelings of frustration and fear. The preparation season is when God is doing miraculous things within us and for us, preparing us for our next blessing and miracle. During the waiting period, the Father is searching our hearts and perfecting our flaws that we may or may not even recognize. God is a God of order, timing, and seasons. "The Lord declares: "For my thoughts are not your thoughts, neither are your ways my ways" (Isa. 55:8). So if we are in the waiting season, two things are taking place: the Father is doing a great work within us, or the time has not come for the very thing we may be waiting for to come to fruition, or both simultaneously. However, the Father gives us instructions on how to stand the test of time and wait on Him. Scripture tells us to:

➢ Wait on the Lord and be of good courage. (Ps. 3:6)
➢ For the vision is yet for an appointed time. (Hab. 2:3)
➢ Lean not on our own understanding. (Prov. 3:5)
➢ Whatever you ask for in prayer, believe that you have received it, and it will be yours. (Mark 11:24)
➢ Let us not be weary in doing good, for at the proper time we will reap a harvest if we do not give up. (Gal. 6:9)
➢ Be still before the Lord and wait patiently for him; do not fret when people succeed in their ways, (Ps. 37:7)
➢ Be strong, do not fear; your God will come. (Isa. 35:4)

It's Worth the Wait

"And we boast in the hope of the glory of God. Not only so, but we also glory in our sufferings, because we know that suffering produces perseverance; perseverance, character; and character, hope. And hope does not put us to shame, because God's love has been poured out into our hearts through the Holy Spirit, who has been given to us." (Rom. 5:2–5)

Patience is a Virtue

"Wait patiently for the Lord. Be brave and courageous. Yes, wait patiently for the LORD." (Ps. 27:14)

Lesson IX

The Number Seven's Perfection and Completion A Time of Rest

"On the seventh day, God had finished his work
of creation, so he rested from all his work."
(Gen. 2:2)

(Jehovah - Sabaoth) The Lord of Host

Introduction:

Numerology is one of the holistic arts of the earth, and numbers in the Bible are used as symbols. Every number has a certain power, which is expressed both by its symbol to denote its representation and by its connection to universal principles. Numbers have relationships with all things in nature, thus making them supremely powerful symbolic expressions. In this lesson, we will explore numbers one through seven; however, we will delve deeper into the number seven, which represents perfection and completion. The spiritual meaning of the numbers presented below are but a glimpse into the spiritual potential each one holds.

Objective:

The Bible, as a whole, was originally divided into seven major divisions: the Law; the Prophet; the Writings, or Psalms; the Gospels and Acts; the General Epistles; the Epistles of Paul; and the book of Revelation. The total number of originally inspired books was forty-nine, or 7 x 7, demonstrating the absolute perfection of the Word of God.

Mission:

"There is a time for everything, and a season for every activity under the heavens." (Eccles. 3:1)

The Spiritual Significance of Numbers 1–7

1—One, also called unit, unity, and multiplicative. It is also the first of the infinite sequence of natural numbers. The number 1 is only divisible by itself. It symbolizes in the Bible the unity and primacy, and the oneness of the Godhead: "The Father, the Son and the Holy Spirit and these three are one." God said to Moses, "I Am Who I Am" (Exod. 3:14.)

2—The number 2 represents a union, division, or the verification of facts by witnesses.

A man and woman, though two in number, are made one in marriage (Gen. 2:23–24). The Bible tells us that two are better than one for agreement.

3—Three, the Trinity of God and the triune of man: "Though one may be overpowered, two can defend themselves, a cord of three strands is not easily broken" (Eccles. 4:12; NIV).

4—Derives from God's "creation." God created the entire material universe on the fourth day: sun, moon, and stars, and the earth's galaxy-controlling time, days, years, and seasons (Gen. 14).

5—The number 5 symbolizes God's goodness and favor toward man, and multiplied by itself, which is twenty-five times greater. Man has five fingers, five senses, and five toes. Thus is the number of God's grace: "For from His fullness we have all received, grace upon grace" (John 1:16).

6—Man was created on the sixth day (Gen. 1:27–31). The number 6 symbolizes man and human weakness, and the evils of Satan and the manifestation of sin. (See more of the number six in Lesson X).

7—The number 7 is the foundation of God's Word. Seven is the number of completeness and perfection both spiritually and physically. It derives much of its meaning from being tied directly to God's creation of all things; He completed and perfected all things including Man. And on the seventh day God rested. "Through Him, all things were made; without Him, nothing was made that has been made"(John 1:3).

The Sevens

The number seven representing the Seven Spirits of God: (Isa. 11:2–3/Rev. 3:1, 4:5, and 5:6)

➢ Love
➢ Righteousness

- ➤ Knowledge
- ➤ Wisdom
- ➤ Faith
- ➤ Hope
- ➤ Judgment

Seven Kinds of Death in Scripture

Throughout scripture, death means separation; and at times, it means inability to produce. It does not mean cessation or annihilation of life. Death is first mentioned in Genesis where God promised Adam he would die if he disobeyed God and ate the forbidden fruit (Gen. 2:16–17). When Adam ate the forbidden fruit, he immediately died spiritually, in that his relationship with God was severed (3:1–7), and he later died physically (Gen. 5:5). If Adam had continued in his state of spiritual death, he would have been in danger of being separated from God forever in the Lake of Fire, which is the Second Death (Rev. 20:11–15). Adam was made spiritually alive again when he accepted God's provision for him (Gen. 3:21). It was Adam's single act of sin in the garden that brought both spiritual and physical death upon the entire human race (Rom. 5:12; 1 Cor. 15:22). The term *death* is also used to refer to Sarah's inability to procreate (Rom. 4:19–21), the inability to produce divine good (James 2:26), the unbeliever's positional death in Adam (1 Cor. 15:21–22), the believer's positional death in Christ (1 Cor. 15:21–22), and the believer who is living a carnal life and is out of fellowship with God (James 1:14–15). The following list should prove helpful:

1. *Spiritual Death* (separation from God in time: Gen. 2:16–17; Eph. 2:1).Mankind's spiritual separation from God because of Adam's sin in the Garden.
2. *The Second Death* (the perpetuation of spiritual death into eternity: Rev. 20:12–15). Forever in the Lake of Fire: the devil, his followers, and the unbeliever.

3. *Physical Death* (the separation of the soul from the body: Eccles 12:7; 2 Cor. 5:8).Adam's single act of sin bought physical death upon the human race.

4. *Sexual Death* (the inability to procreate: Rom. 4:19–21). Sarah's barren womb.

5. *Operational Death* (the inability to produce divine good: James 2:26). Attempting to function outside of the Spirit Man and operate without faith.

6. *Positional Death* in Adam (Rom. 5:12; 1 Cor. 15:22), and in Christ (Rom. 6:8; 1 Cor. 15:22; Col. 3:3). The unbeliever's positional death through Adam; the believers positional death in Christ.

7. *Carnal Death* (this is the believer's out of fellowship with God, operating according to his sinful nature: Rom. 8:6, 13; James 1:14–15; Rev. 3:1; Luke 15:24, 32).

Steven R. Cook

The Blood Seat of Mercy

Jesus shed his blood in seven bodily places for the redemption of mankind. (See Lesson III)

- Freedom
- Healing
- Peace
- Prosperity
- Dominion
- Authority
- Restoration

The Seven Feasts in Honoring the Lord (Lev. 23)

We are sanctioned by God to meet with Him three times a year and stand before Him with an offering. Matthew 13:8 says,

"If we sow into good soil, it will produce a harvest of thirty, sixty, hundred times greater."

The Seven Feasts are combined into three appointed seasons: spring, summer, and fall. These seasons were established for the children of God to be reminded of the blood sacrifice, and reflect, repent, and honor our Lord.

Passover—Appointed Spring Season: Thirty-Fold Blessing

- Passover—Jesus' death, The sacrificial lamb (Exod. 11–12)
- Unleavened Bread—Jesus the Bread of Life (John 6:35)
- First Fruits—Guides us to the Savior (1 Cor.15:2–23)

Feast of Weeks—Appointed Summer Season: Sixty-Fold Blessing

- Pentecost—The Holy Spirit arrives (Acts 2:1–4)

Feast of Tabernacle—Appointed Fall Season: Hundred-Fold Blessing

- Feast of Trumpets—Return to the Lord (1 Thess. 4:16)
- Day of Atonement—The Word became Flesh (5:8–15)
- Feast of Tabernacle—Jesus' fellowship and rein with mankind (John 1:14)

Seven Blessing of the Atonement (See Lesson XI)

The Lord showers us with spiritual blessings, when we honor Him on His holy appointed day.

- A double portion
- Financial abundance

- Restoration
- Miracles
- God's divine presence
- Blessing upon your family
- Deliverance

Seven Mountains of Purpose (See Lesson XIII)

Whichever mountain we possess, we need to be fruitful for the kingdom of God.

- Religion
- Family
- Education
- Government
- Media, TV, Screenwriters
- Arts, Entertainment, Sports
- Business

Seven Mountains of Life (See Lesson XIII)

Our trails are not meant to break us; they are meant to shape us!

- Family
- Work
- Finances
- Health
- Marriage
- Children
- Affliction

The Seven Principles of Prayer (See Lesson VIII)

- Honor
- Confession
- Agreement
- Repentance
- Forgiveness
- Rebuke the Enemy
- Praise and Worship

Forgiveness

The ultimate gift to give to yourself is to forgive others.

"Then came Peter to him and said, Lord, how often shall my brother sin against me, and I forgive him? till seven times? Jesus saith unto him, I say not unto thee, Until seven times: but, Until seventy times seven." (Matt. 18:21–22)

Restoration (Prov. 24:16)

"For the righteous falls seven times and rises again, but the wicked stumble in times of calamity."

Praise and Worship (Ps. 119:164)

King David praised God seven times a day.

Restitution (Prov. 6:30–31)

"Men do not despise a thief, if he steal to satisfy his soul when he is hungry; But if he be found, he shall restore sevenfold; he shall give all the substance of his house."

Debt Free (Deut. 15:1)

Debt cancellation every seven years: "At the end of every seven years, you shall grant remission of debts."

Prosperity and Famine (Gen. 41:51 –54)

"Joseph named the firstborn Manasseh, 'For,' he said, 'God has made me forget all my trouble, and all my father's household.' He named the second Ephraim, 'For,' he said, 'God has made me fruitful in the land of my affliction.' When the seven years of plenty which had been in the land of Egypt came to an end, and the seven years of famine began to come, just as Joseph had said, then there was famine in all the lands, but in all the land of Egypt there was bread."

Laboring (Gen. 29:20)

Jacob gave seven years of service for wife Rachel to his uncle Laban said, "It is better that I give her to you than to give her to another man; stay with me. So Jacob served seven years for Rachel and they seemed to him but a few days because of his love for her."

The Walls of Jericho (Josh. 6: 1–5)

"Now the gates of Jericho were securely barred because of the Israelites. No one went out and no one came in. Then the LORD said to Joshua, 'See, I have delivered Jericho into your hands, along with its king and its fighting men. March around the city once with all the armed men. Do this for six days. Have seven priests carry trumpets of rams' horns in front of the ark. On the seventh day, march around the city seven times, with the priests blowing the trumpets. When you hear them sound a long blast on the trumpets, have the whole army give a loud shout; then the wall of the city will collapse and the army will go up, everyone straight in.'"

Naaman Healed of Leprosy (2 Kings 5:1–9)

Now Naaman was commander of the army of the king of Aram. He was a great man in the sight of his master and highly regarded because through him, the LORD had given victory to Aram. He was a valiant soldier, but he had leprosy.

Now bands of raiders from Aram had gone out and had taken captive a young girl from Israel, and she served Naaman's wife. She said to her mistress, "If only my master would see the prophet who is in Samaria! He would cure him of his leprosy."

Naaman went to his master and told him what the girl from Israel had said. "By all means, go," the king of Aram replied. "I will send a letter to the king of Israel." So Naaman left, taking with him ten talents of silver, six thousand shekels of gold, and ten sets of clothing. The letter that he took to the king of Israel read: "With this letter, I am sending my servant Naaman to you so that you may cure him of his leprosy."

As soon as the king of Israel read the letter, he tore his robes and said, "Am I God? Can I kill and bring back to life? Why does this fellow send someone to me to be cured of his leprosy? See how he is trying to pick a quarrel with me!" When Elisha, the man of God, heard that the king of Israel had torn his robes, he sent him this message: "Why have you torn your robes? Have the man come to me and he will know that there is a prophet in Israel." So Naaman went with his horses and chariots and stopped at the door of Elisha's house. Elisha sent a messenger to say to him, "Go, wash yourself seven times in the Jordan, and your flesh will be restored and you will be cleansed."

Elijah Prays for Rain (1 Kings 18:41–45)

Then Elijah said to Ahab, "Go get something to eat and drink, for I hear a mighty rainstorm coming!" So Ahab went to eat and drink. But Elijah climbed to the top of Mount Carmel and bowed low to the ground and prayed with his face between his knees. Then he said to his servant, "Go and look out toward the sea." The servant went and looked, then returned to Elijah and said, "I didn't see anything. Seven times Elijah told him to go and look. Finally the seventh time, his servant told him, "I saw a little cloud about the size of a man's hand rising from the sea."

Daniel's Prayer Tied Up (Dan. 10:12–13)

Then he said to me, "Do not be afraid, Daniel, for from the first day that you set your heart on understanding this and on humbling yourself before your God, your words were heard, and I have come in response to your words. But of the kingdom of Persia was withstanding me for twenty-one days; then behold, Michael, one of the chief princes, came to help me, for I had been left there with the kings of Persia."

Seven Times Greater Offering onto the Lord (Job 42:8)

"So now take seven bulls and seven rams and go to my servant Job and sacrifice a burnt offering for yourselves. My servant Job will pray for you, and I will accept his prayer and not deal with you according to your folly. You have not spoken the truth about me, as my servant Job has."

The Human Body Perfected

There are seven octillion atoms in the human body which super exceeds the amount of stars in the universe. The estimate of seven trillion is seven billion, billion, billion atoms per human body. The human body has more than the number of stars in the galaxy, which sit at three hundred billion; the sum of mankind is greater than the stars (7,000,000,000,000,000,000,000,000,000)!

Sevens in Nature

The sevens of God can also be observed in the things of nature. It appears that the physics and chemistry of nature are structured on such a base system. An example that almost everyone can relate to is music. All the songs you hear on the radio are based on a musical system of just seven major notes:

Notice that the seven notes repeat, with the eighth key a higher octave of the first as you go up (or down) the keyboard. All other minor notes, sharps, and flats, fit within the structure of the basic seven musical notes.

If you pass sunlight through a prism, it produces seven colors—the three primary colors and four secondary ones:

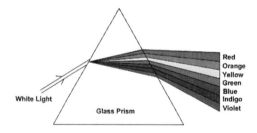

In the realm of minerals and geochemistry, there are seven crystal systems:

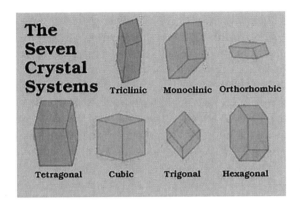

Here is a picture of example minerals from each of the seven systems:

Even the Periodic Table of the known elements appears to have seven levels of periodicity:

IA																	**0**
1 H	**II A**											**III A**	**IVA**	**VA**	**VI A**	**VII A**	2 He
3 Li	4 Be											5 B	6 C	7 N	8 O	9 F	10 Ne
11 Na	12 Mg	**IIIB**	**IVB**	**VB**	**VIB**	**VIIB**	——— VIII ———			**IB**	**IIB**	13 Al	14 Si	15 P	16 S	17 Cl	18 Ar
19 K	20 Ca	21 Sc	22 Ti	23 V	24 Cr	25 Mn	26 Fe	27 Co	28 Ni	29 Cu	30 Zn	31 Ga	32 Ge	33 As	34 Se	35 Br	36 Kr
37 Rb	38 Sr	39 Y	40 Zr	41 Nb	42 Mo	43 Tc	44 Ru	45 Rh	46 Pd	47 Ag	48 Cd	49 In	50 Sn	51 Sb	52 Te	53 I	54 Xe
55 Cs	56 Ba	57 *La	72 Hf	73 Ta	74 W	75 Re	76 Os	77 Ir	78 Pt	79 Au	80 Hg	81 Tl	82 Pb	83 Bi	84 Po	85 At	86 Rn
87 Fr	88 Ra	89 +Ac	104 Rf	105 Ha	106 106	107 107	108 108	109 109	110 110								

Periodic Table of the Elements

* Lanthanide Series	58 Ce	59 Pr	60 Nd	61 Pm	62 Sm	63 Eu	64 Gd	65 Tb	66 Dy	67 Ho	68 Er	69 Tm	70 Yb	71 Lu
+ Actinide Series	90 Th	91 Pa	92 U	93 Np	94 Pu	95 Am	96 Cm	97 Bk	98 Cf	99 Es	100 Fm	101 Md	102 No	103 Lr

Seven Special Spices (Deut. 8: 7–8)

Since the fruiting of the seven fruits is linked to our body's health, it is not surprising that these seven kinds comprise a wealth of nutrients and medicinal properties.

- **Wheat**—strengthens the body and increases mother's milk.
- **Barley**—a recent study by the FDA evidenced that barley reduces cholesterol and risk of coronary disease.
- **Grapes**—grape-seed oil nourishes the skin while also containing a very high content of antioxidants that help in eliminating free radicals. Grapes possess a diuretic quality, yet they are very nutritive replete with vitamins A, B, and C while also treating blood and energy deficiency.
- **Figs**—modern science affirms the nutritional benefits of figs. They are very rich in minerals especially potas-

sium, iron, and calcium; and they contain omega-3 and omega-6 fatty acids. Figs also contain phytosterols which inhibit the absorption of dietary cholesterol, thus decreasing the total levels of cholesterol. Moreover, they may help prevent certain types of cancers.

- **Pomegranates**—pomegranates boost our immune system. Pomegranate seed oil causes cancer cells to self-destruct. The juice of the fruit is toxic to most breast cancer cells, yet has almost no effect on healthy cells. Pomegranate juice has also been proven to decrease heart disease by decreasing LDL (bad cholesterol) and increased HDL (good cholesterol).
- **Olives**—olive oil is the foundation of most Mediterranean foods. Maimonides explains that olive oil cleanses the liver and loosens stools. Drinking a teaspoon of olive oil every morning before eating can help prevent stones in the urinary tract. Olive oil protects against heart disease by lowering blood pressure and has strong antibacterial properties. It also contains several antioxidants to help fight cancer.
- **Dates**—connected with the digestive system and heals intestinal illnesses.

Health and Wellness Perfected

The Old Testament' mention of the seven spices is not incidental. Rather, these foods are central to healthy eating and living. Incorporating the seven spices into our diet can promote our well-being and help us connect to the land that God has provided for us His children. Each of the seven spices contains deep lessons about God and our spiritual lives. Every time we eat them, we have the opportunity to tune into their spiritual messages, eat consciously, and bring the world a step closer to its perfected state.

Scripture: "Therefore you are able to be perfect, as your Heavenly Father is perfect." (Matt. 5:48)

Lesson X

Satan Already Defeated

"So you know Jesus of Nazareth, how God anointed
him with the Holy Spirit and with power, and how
He went about doing good and healing all who were
oppressed by the devil, for God was with Him."
(Acts 10:38)

(Jehovah - Machsi) The Lord My Refuge

Introduction:

The devil attacks the mind and personality traits of mankind; and because the mind is a set of cognitive faculties including our consciousness, imagination, perception, thinking, judgment, and memory enhanced and stimulated by our five senses, both the body and soul of mankind is targeted by the enemy. This is why God says, "Meditate on the Word day and night to be prosperous." Because the enemy can invade our thoughts, which in return, causes one to lose self- control over their actions and emotions. The devil cannot, however, influence or control the Spirit of mankind; that is God's territory. John 4:4 tells us, "He who dwells within is greater than he that is in the world." This is why Satan works "overtime" every second of the day to cause what is known as the "Seven Ds" in our lives: destruction, disappointment, distractions, dismantling, disagreements, disengagements, and disapproval.

The Enemy's Cause and Effect upon Mankind

1. **Destruction**—the action or process of causing so much damage to something that it no longer exists or cannot be repaired.
   - ➤ health, marriages, family, businesses, career
2. **Disappointment**—the feeling of sadness or displeasure caused by the non-fulfillment of one's hopes or expectations.
   - ➤ depression, drugs, obsessive drinking, addictions, abuse, suicidal ideations, lust
3. **Distractions**—a thing that prevents someone from giving full attention to something else.
   - ➤ unhealthy relationships, social media, television, video games, gambling, unproductive, gossiping, debauchery
4. **Dismantling**—take apart, pull apart, pull to pieces, disassemble, break up, break down, strip down.

> character, integrity, identity, self-esteem, emotions, reputation, matters of the heart

5. **Disagreements**—lack of consensus or approval, variance, controversy, discord, contention, division.

> separation from family, friends, colleagues, envy, jealousy, affliction

6. **Disengagement**—the action or process of withdrawing from involvement in a particular activity, situation, or group.

> racism, bigotry, stereotypes, hatred, biased, prideful

7. **Disapproval**—possession or expression of an unfavorable opinion: disapprobation, objection, dislike.

> judgment

The enemy can influence the actions and perceptions of man. This is why God specifically informs us to "renew our minds day and night in His Word." So we can be steadfast and unmovable, able to stand against the wiles of the devil. "The Bully" influences are never good or for our good; it always has a negative, devastating outcome. Scripture tells us, "Be sober, watchful, and vigilant." We must become aware of our surroundings, and begin to observe situations and actions of others. Not in a judgmental way, but with the knowledge and wisdom of God. Ask the Lord to enlighten your understanding because the enemy is continuously lurking around, looking for someone to negatively influence and devour through us or toward us.

Objective:

"For we do not wrestle against flesh and blood, but against the rulers, but against the authorities, against the cosmic powers over the present darkness, against the spiritual forces of evil in heavenly places." (Eph. 6:12–13)

Mission:

"You believe that; God is one, you do well. Even the demons believe—and shudder!" (James 2:19)

The "Bully's" Character Profile

Lucifer, Satan, Demon, Serpent, Beelzebub, Fallen Angel, Devil, Accuser, Adversary, Father of lies, Antichrist, Dragon, Enemy, Legion, Accuser of our brethren, Angel of the bottomless pit, Crooked serpent, Evil spirit, Lying spirit, Murderer, Prince of this world, Prince of the power of this world, Prince of the darkness of this world, Tempter, The God of this world, Unclean spirit, Spirit that works in the children of disobedience, The Wicked One!

Appearances

Impersonator of diversion, perversion, negative persuasion, sickness, poverty, anger, jealousy, envy, betrayal, unforgiveness, debauchery, addictions, mental health, lies, depression, hatred, racism, bigotry, fear, struggles with gender identity, adultery, supremacy, murder, and all negative personality traits. Satan can influence and/or control mankind's actions both mentally and physically. The adversary can have an influence over those who are saved in Christ Jesus that are not aware; not mediating on the Word day and night; not following the principles of God; and not being sober, watchful, and vigilant. It's crucial to be knowledgeable that the Serpent can influence those in Christ as well, but can take full control over those who are not saved in Christ Jesus.

Role of Satan

To rob us of our purpose and the promises of God from the time we are born; kill us before our time; and destroy every person, place, or thing we come into contact with.

What's at Stake?

Purpose! The enemy does not want us to fulfill our destiny for the kingdom. This is why many of us are soul searching for purpose and why there are so many obstacles and hurdles to jump over in finding and fulfilling purpose. The enemy is constantly trying to block mankind from learning the truth about the Father and Jesus Christ's blood sacrifice for our sins. The devil targets our identity and creates blinders so we won't walk in our God-given purpose and power. He does not want us to know who we truly are and what we represent as children of the kingdom of God.

Background History

Lucifer was the most beautiful of all angels and music filled the heavens through him. He betrayed God; he wanted to become God and take over heaven because he became jealous of the love that God has for mankind. Lucifer cursed God, stating "he was going to take over the Throne of Heaven. He was thrown out of heaven by God; and took a third of the angels with him" (Ezek. 28:13).

Scripture: "And He said to them, "I was watching Satan fall from heaven like lightning." (Luke 10:18)

(Jehovah - Melech 'Olam) King Forever

Mark of the Beast

The number six in the kingdom of God represents mankind because God completed the triune of mankind on the sixth day,

"The Lord formed man from the dust of the ground, and breathed into his nostrils the breath of life; and man became a living soul" (Gen. 2:7). Satan's mark 666 interpreted in the kingdom means: man, man, man; and Satan hates mankind! He despises the whole entire triune of man: body, soul and spirit. The devil has marked mankind and his mission is to rob, kill, and destroy the triune of man on earth by any means necessary!

John 1:38

Scripture: "The one that practices sin is of the devil; for the devil has sinned from the beginning the Son of God appeared for this purpose, to destroy the works of the devil."

Spirit of the Bully

a. (noun) Uses strength or power to harm or intimidate those who are weaker, persecutor, oppressor, tyrant, tormentor, and intimidator.

b. (verb) Uses superior strength or influence to intimidate (someone), typically to force him or her to do what one wants.

Scripture: "I write to you, fathers, because you have known Him who is from the beginning. I write to you, young men, because you have overcome the wicked one. I write to you, little children, because you have known the Father. I have written to you, fathers, because you have known Him who is from the beginning. I have written to you, young men, because you are strong, and the word of God abides in you, and you have overcome the wicked one." (Rom. 16:20)

The Bully Influences the Good Strengths of Mankind

Whatever strengths or weaknesses one may possess, the enemy will try and influence it in a negative way.

Example:

If the strength is enjoying helping others, the enemy will create a multiple of extreme situations where one may begin helping others too much that they neglect their responsibilities and family to the point of becoming tired, miserable, weak, sick, or even depressed. Others will not seem appreciative and begin to take the kindness for weakness to the point of helping others is no longer desirable.

The deception here is to rob us of acts of kindness, which is what as stewards of the kingdom we should be doing. The goal of the adversary is to inflict isolation and have the individual stop helping others. The person becomes bitter because they are burnt out and begin to use the Gift of Kindness in a negative way. Experiencing betrayal and hurt on multiple occasions causes one to revert to self-preservation, which can lead to unforgiveness, selfishness and manipulation. Now what was once sincere acts of kindness is replaced with undesirable acts and despair.

The Bully Influences the Weakness of Mankind

Example:

If the weakness is having a difficulty telling people no, the devil will target that area and present a numerous amount of situations that will make it difficult to say no to; and down the road, this causes the individual to be placed in situations that affect them to the point of being taken advantage of, participating in immoral acts, being mistreated, abused, and loosing self-control.

The deception here is not being able to say no to certain situations can cause one to compromise oneself in a variety of undesirable ways, situations, and circumstances.

The Bully's Major Deception

The Bully's main tactic is to get us to experience fear in every situation of our lives because fear disconnects us from God. Back in the Garden of Eden when Eve was deceived by the Serpent and Adam disobeyed God, the first characteristic they displayed and felt was fear. Fear is the opposition of not having faith in God. The Lord asked Adam, "Where are you?" and Adam responded, "We hid because we were naked and afraid."

The devil loves to influence us through fear because if we are experiencing fear, we are not trusting God, and we begin to perform from our body's five senses or from the soul using our own perceptions, beliefs, and physical strength as opposed to trusting God and allowing the Holy Spirit to guide, lead, and strengthen our spirit.

2 Timothy 1:7

Scripture: "For God has not given us a spirit of fear but of power, love and a sound mind."

How to Defeat the Bully

1. Believe that he is real and out to destroy you; but if you resist him, he will flee.
2. Meditate on the Word of God.
3. Be sober and vigilant.
4. Listen to your thoughts, and if they don't line up with the Word of God, cast them out!
5. Speak out loud with dominion and authority, **declare what the outcome will be according to God's Word.**
   Examples:
   a) Devil, I rebuke the negative thought(s) of _____ _____ and cast them back into the pits of hell, and they shall not return onto me again!
   b) Lord, I cast down all negative imaginations that do not line up with your Word back into the sea. I bind it, and I loosen it, and whatever I shall bind and loose on earth shall be bound and loosed in heaven!

c) Satan, you have no authority over my mind, body, or soul. I command you to lose me right now today. Let there be light!

d) I rebuke you, Satan, and your deception, trickery, and lies about myself, my family, my purpose, my children, my health, my addictions, my business, my career, and my destiny for the kingdom of God. I shall live and not die; I will not abort or give up because He who dwells in me is greater than he that is in the world, and no weapon that you form against me shall be able to prosper!

In Jesus' Mighty Name! Amen.

6. Apply the principles of God.

7. Have weapons of warfare in place. (See Lesson XI)

Scripture: "But if I cast out demons by the spirit of God, then the kingdom has come upon you." (Matt. 12:28)

"When we wake up in the morning and place our feet on the floor, hell should shake!"

—Joyce Myers

We Are Never Alone

a) God is always with us. "He will never leave you nor forsake you."

b) The Holy Ghost dwells within us, and He is leading and guiding us every day. He awaits for us to acknowledge that He is present within, helping us fight the good fight of faith. The Holy Ghost communicates with the Father on our behalf daily, moaning and groaning for us to be perfected, lacking nothing.

Speak to Him who dwells within:

Example: Holy Ghost, have your way today in my life. Order my steps and direct my path so I will perform the works of the Father and walk in His perfect will.

c) We have warring angels assigned to us daily; acknowledge their presence, put them to work every day. Speak out loud to the angels that encamp around us.

Example: I give the angels that encamp around me the authority to take charge over the enemy that attempts to hinder me in any way today. I shall be prosperous in every way and wherever my feet shall tread, I am a blessing, and I will be a blessing for I am the head and not the tail!

d) The Word of God is active and powerful. Speak it!

e) Remember, because of the blood, we have dominion and authority in Christ Jesus; He is our advocate, going to the Father in our defense every day: His mercy and grace is sufficient. thank Him, praise Him, and worship Him; He is worthy to be praised!

Colossians 1:13

Scripture: "For he rescued us from the domain of the darkness, and transferred us to the kingdom of His beloved Son.
(Jehovah- Hoshe'ah) The Lord Who Saves

1 John 2:13–14

Scripture: "The God of peace will soon crush Satan under your feet, the grace of the Lord Jesus be with you."
(Jehovah - Nissi) The Lord Is My Banner

"The devil's success depends on my ignorance."
—Benny Hinn

Lesson XI

Weapons of Warfare

"For though we walk in the flesh, we do not war
according to the flesh, for the weapons of our warfare
are not of the flesh, but divinely powerful for the
destruction of fortresses." (2 Cor. 10:3–4)

(Jehovah Chereb) Glorious Sword

Introduction:

In the last lesson, you learned about the Bully. In this lesson, you will gain knowledge on the Weapons of Warfare God has provided us with weapons to be victorious and defeat the Devil at all of his tactics when we begin to practice applying the principles of God along with the weapons of warfare in our daily walk with the Lord. Then and only then will we be totally undefeatable in every area of our lives and begin to operate from a kingdom perspective through the Word of God. In doing so, our faith increases, and we become spiritually in tuned with who we are in Christ Jesus. Taking charge of the dominion and authority that we possess, which is what we have been called to do as ambassadors for the kingdom of God and this is how we will bring heaven down to earth!

Objective:

"For the weapons of our warfare are not carnal, but they are mighty in God for pulling down of strong holds." (2 Cor. 10:4)

Mission:

"Put on the whole armor of God, that ye maybe able to stand against the wiles of the devil." (Eph. 6:11)

The Movement

God said, "The weapons of our warfare are not carnal but mighty in Him." God has provided us with tangible weapons of warfare that are spiritual and still active today. Weapons that destroy yokes rebuke the devourer and protect us; allowing us to be victorious right here, right now, today! "God's Word does not return onto him void; but it accomplishes everything that it is sent to do" (Isa. 55:11). "God is not a man that He should lie, nor a son of man, that He should repent." (Num. 23:19). He is God Almighty, the Alpha and the Omega; and whatever God speaks, it will come to pass! Why? Because, it is written: "Man shall not live by bread alone; but by every Word that proceeds out of the mouth of God" (Matt. 4:4). The Holy Bible is our weapon of warfare, filled with God's power, knowledge, wisdom, and instructions.

Words in Action

There are seven components on how to armor ourselves daily through the Word of God.

The Word

    a. meditate on it
    b. know it
    c. use it
    d. agree with it
    e. decree it
    f. confess it
    g. stand on it (don't waiver; stay in faith)

"Revolutionize Your Life and Rewrite Your Future with the Power of Words"

—Dr. Bill Winston

God Always Provides a Blueprint

Look at God's approach with Moses. God leads Moses to Him through the burning bush, speaks to Moses, instructing him on His plan and purpose. God demonstrates to Moses that the rod in his hand was no ordinary rod but was a weapon of warfare that he would use to perform miracles and wonders, and then God paired Moses up with his brother Aaron to encourage him along the way.

God's Principles Demonstrated with Moses

- ✓ God attracts Moses (visually by the burning bush)—Without a vision, the people will perish.
- ✓ God speaks to Moses (auditory stimulation)—Faith comes by hearing the Word of God.
- ✓ God transforms Moses's rod—Weapon of Warfare.
- ✓ God pairs Moses with his brother Aaron (Agreement)—"Two people are better than one, for they can help each other succeed" (Eccles. 4:9).

We read God's principle blue print with Moses. Let's begin to build. "Because greater works shall we do because Jesus goes to the father for us" (John 14:12).

Weapon of Covering

In the Old Testament, God spoke to Moses to speak to the children of Israel and guided them throughout generations to begin making fringes on the corners of their garments, which symbolized guidance and protection for the children of Israel (Num. 15:37–40). The design of the garments was the beginning stage and formation of the tallit (a prayer shawl).

The tallit is a four-cornered prayer shawl with specifically knotted fringes on the corners, also symbolic for healing power in the New Testament. Jesus wore a tallit, and scripture tells us that when a certain woman with an issue of blood touched the hem of Jesus' garment, that sickness left the woman's body; and she was instantly healed from a blood disorder that she had suffered from for twelve years (Mark 5).

Divine Protection

"He that dwelleth in the secret place of the most high shall abide under the shadow of the almighty." (Ps. 91:1)

"When we cover ourselves with the tallit, we are under God's divine protection. We enter into "the secret place" (Matt. 6:6).

The Intruder

The human mind is a transmitter, processing electromagnetic waves that carry messages or signals, like a radio or television. Therefore, at any time, both verbal and nonverbal communicators can pass through and connect to our brains without our permission.

For example:

A walkie-talkie, once it's connected to a channel, can intercept a conversation, transmit information, or just listen in without other parties being aware. This is what the devil does. He attacks our minds and listens in on our thoughts, most inner secrets, and conversations. Then the devil devises an attack on how he plans to rob, kill, and destroy us at any means necessary, showing no mercy! This is why God instructs us to renew our minds and meditate on the Word day and night so we can be prosperous, casting down imaginations that don't align with the Word of God because the mind can play tricks on you, right? No! Not our minds. The devil is the trickster; he is the mastermind of tricks and deception.

Thinking Made Perfect

Regulating our thoughts and filtering the positive from the negative is detrimental to our purpose.

Question: How do we regulate our thought process?

Answer: Now that we know what the enemy's first attack will be, our next step is to cover ourselves during prayer every day with a tallit; and "Be sober, be vigilant because the adversary the devil, as a roaring lion, walketh about, seeking whom he may devour" (1 Pet. 5:8). God has given us the tallit as a weapon of warfare to keep the enemy from attacking our minds during prayer.

The Secret Place

"But thou, when thou prayest, enter into thy *closet,* and when thou hast *shut thy door, pray to thy Father which is in secret*; and thy Father which seeth in secret *shall reward thee openly*" (Matt. 6:6).

How We Enter Into the Secret Place

First, enter into the *closet;* place the tallit over your head.

Second, *shut the door*; pull the sides together, like closing a curtain, to cover your face; this is closing the door.

Third, *pray to the Father.* The door being shut indicates that you have entered the secret place and communicates to the adversary that he cannot interfere within our thoughts and prayers. He is forbidden!

Closing the door is the "secrete place"

Gifts in the Secret Place

"God rewards us openly" because now the devil cannot intercept. He does not know what to rob, kill, or destroy. It's a secret shared only with the Father, the Son, and the Holy Ghost.

Pray, Pray, Pray

a. Speak out loud and follow the Seven Principles on prayer. (see Lesson VIII)
b. Pray without ceasing. (Never stop)
c. Pray with a tallit. (Enter the secret place)
d. Pray in tongues. (Ask the Holy Spirit to anoint you with the gift of praying in tongues)

Scripture: "And pray in the Spirit on all occasions with all kinds of prayers and request. With this in mind, be alert and always keep praying for the Lord's people" (Eph. 6:18).

Weapon for Safe Travels

In the Book of Deuteronomy, Moses gives his farewell address to the children of Israel. Knowing that they would soon enter into the Promise Land without him, Moses was responsible for reminding them of the covenant that was made between their parents and the Lord. Moses teaches the future generation about the works and Words of God, and describes a weapon of warfare to the children of Israel, giving them reassurance that they are covered and protected by the Lord always.

Mezuzah

The Mezuzah

The word *mezuzah* means, doorpost. It's a parchment scroll with a handwritten scribe, incased, that is placed on the doorpost. Moses instructed the children of Israel to "Place one on every door and blessed shall you be when you come in, blessed shall you be when you go out" (Deut. 28:6).

Educate the Seeds

The mezuzah is a weapon of warfare for all generations to come. "Fix these words of mine in your hearts and minds; tie them as symbols on your hands and bind them on your foreheads. Teach them to your children, talking about them when you sit at home and when you walk along the road, when you lie down and when you get up. Write them on the doorframes of your houses and on your gates, so that your days and the days of your children may be many in the land the LORD swore to give your ancestors, as many as the days that the heavens are above the earth." (Deut. 11:18–21)

The Gate is Open

Every year, God opens up the Book of Life which has the names of His children inscribed that will live with Him forever in eternity. The Book of Life is open on Rosh Hashanah, known as the beginning of the New Year on the Hebrew calendar. And for a period of ten days, known as the ten days of Awe, the Feast of Trumpets, the Lord requires that His children reflect on the past year by honoring Him, repenting, and performing good deeds before resealing our fate. Every year, God provides an opportunity during this season for those who have not confessed Jesus Christ as their personal Savior to have their names written in the Book of Life. This gives the unbeliever the opportunity to repent and confess Jesus Christ as their personal Savior and seal their fate in eternity. God considers this time of the year to be the holiest, and during this season, God's blessings are poured out the greatest.

At One with God

However, on the tenth day, the Day of Atonement, the Lord's holiest day, He commands His children to be obedient. "The LORD said to Moses, 'The tenth day of this seventh month is the Day of Atonement. Hold a sacred assembly and deny yourselves, and present a food offering to the LORD. Do not do any work on that day, because it is the Day of Atonement, when atonement is made for you before the LORD your God. Those who do not deny themselves on that day must be cut off from their people. I will destroy from among their people anyone who does any work on that day. You shall do no work at all. This is to be a lasting ordinance for the generations to come, wherever you live. It is a day of Sabbath rest for you, and you must deny yourselves. From the evening of the ninth day of the month until the following evening you are to observe your Sabbath" (Lev. 23:26–32; NIV).

The Lord Gives Further Instructions about the Day of Atonement (Joel 2:12–14)

"Now therefore, says the Lord, 'Turn to Me with your heart, with fasting, with weeping, and with mourning.' So rend your heart, and not your garments; Return to the Lord your God, for He is gracious and merciful, slow to anger, and of great kindness; and He relents from doing harm. Who knows if He will turn and relent, and leave a blessing behind Him—a grain offering and a drink offering for the Lord your God."

Atonement: The Lord's Day, Keep It Holy.

➤ no work
➤ fast

➤ repent
➤ give an offering onto the Lord
➤ wear white garments (sign of purity)
➤ pray, read the Torah, Book of Ester, Psalms 27
➤ no extra-curricular activities
➤ refrain from sexual intercourse

The Great Exchange

The Day of Atonement is a time to commemorate and show reverence to the Father. It is an ordinance established by the Lord to be kept forever. In return, the Lord, promises His children Seven Blessings. Oh Saints, what a wonderful God we serve! In the Book of Joel 2, the Seven Blessings of the Day of Atonement are poured out.

"The Lord will answer and say to His people, 'Behold, I will send you grain and new wine oil, And you will be satisfied by them; Fear not, O land; Be glad and rejoice, for the Lord has done marvelous things! Rejoice in the Lord your God.'"

First Atonement Blessing: A Double Portion

He has given you the former rain faithfully,
And He will cause the rain to come down for you—
The former rain, and the latter rain in the first month.

Second Atonement Blessing: Financial Abundance

The threshing floors shall be full of wheat, and the vats shall overflow with new wine and oil.

Third Atonement Blessing: Restoration

So I will restore to you the years that the swarming locust has eaten,
The crawling locust,
The consuming locust,
And the chewing locust,

My great army which I sent among you.

Fourth Atonement Blessing: Miracles
You shall eat in plenty and be satisfied,
And praise the name of the LORD your God,
Who has dealt wondrously with you;
And My people shall never be put to shame.

Fifth Atonement Blessing: God's Divine Presence
Then you shall know that I am in the midst of Israel:
I am the LORD your God
And there is no other.
My people shall never be put to shame.

Sixth Atonement Blessing: Blessing upon Your Family
And it shall come to pass afterward
That I will pour out My Spirit on all flesh;
Your sons and your daughters shall prophesy,
Your old men shall dream dreams,
Your young men shall see visions.
And also on My menservants and on My maidservants
I will pour out My Spirit in those days.
And I will show wonders in the heavens and in the earth:
Blood and fire and pillars of smoke.
The sun shall be turned into darkness,
And the moon into blood,
Before the coming of the great and awesome day of the LORD.

Seventh Atonement Blessing: Deliverance
And it shall come to pass
That whoever calls on the name of the LORD
Shall be saved.

Inspired by: Dr. Steve Munsey

Shofar

Weapon of Warfare

The "shofar" is a ram's horn that is sounded during the month of Elul, known as the Feast of Trumpets, the season of Rosh Hashanah up until the Day of Atonement (Yom Kippur). It is mentioned numerous times in the Bible. The shofar, in the Old Testament, was used during religious ceremonies as a battle signal; it's a ram's horn that is blown like a trumpet observed during the Feast of Trumpets. The shofar is symbolic of the Torah, which is the first five books of Moses from Genesis to Deuteronomy. The shofar is blown yearly as a sign of the coming of our Lord and being victorious during times of tribulations.

In Remembrance

> ➤ Blow the shofar on Rosh Hashanah, which is the Feast of Trumpet: reveals our soon-returning Savior. (1 Thess. 4:16)
> ➤ Blow the shofar on the Day of Atonement: guides us to understand how the Word became flesh. (Rom. 5:8–15)
> ➤ Blow the shofar when at war and oppressed by the enemy, the Lord will remember and come to our rescue; the enemy will be defeated! (Num. 10:9)

Jehovah Shiloh – The one to whom it belongs.

Forever Means Forever

At sundown on the Day of Atonement, God closes the Book of Life until the following year. Once the Lord has written our names in His Book; it's there for eternity!

"He who over comes shall be clothed in white garments, and I will not blot out his name from the Book of Life; but I will confess his name before My Father and before His Angels." (Rev. 3:5)

Numbers 6:24-26

Scripture: "The LORD bless thee, and keep thee:

The LORD make his face shine upon thee, and be gracious unto thee:

The LORD lift up his countenance upon thee, and give thee peace."

Shalom

Go Back to School

Final Exam

"The student is not above the teacher, but everyone
who is fully trained will be like their teacher."
(Luke 6:40)

(God the Alpha and Omega) The Beginning and the End

Name:_____Date: _____

Go Back to School: Final Exam

1. Did God instruct us, "to seek His kingdom first"?
    TRUE   FALSE

2. Is God a God of order, cycles, seasons, and principles?
    TRUE   FALSE

3. Are we supposed to take everything to the Lord in prayer?
    TRUE   FALSE

4. Is tithing in the kingdom of God like an investment, and God promises a lucrative return and an abundance of blessings?
    TRUE   FALSE

5. In scripture, God quotes that if we don't have _____, it's impossible to please Him.
    A. Freedom   B. Focus
    C. Friends   D. Faith
    E. All of the above

6. What should we do with the Word of God day and night to be prosperous?

7. Is it crucial that we write down our visions and dreams?
    TRUE   FALSE

8. Does scripture tell us confession is good for our souls?
    TRUE   FALSE

9. What is the Agreement Principle?

10. Can people perish from lack of knowledge?
    TRUE   FALSE

11. Where should we place the mezuzah, and what is its symbolic purpose?

12. Is fasting a principle?
    TRUE   FALSE

13. What does the bread and wine symbolize for Holy Communion?

14. Does scripture tell us to pray continually?
    TRUE   FALSE

15. What are the Seven Principles within the Lord's Prayer?

16. Explain the Expectation Principle?

17. Which terms describe "patience"?
    A. Longsuffering   B. Delay
    C. Tolerance   D. Peace
    E. All of the above

18. What does the number "seven" mean spiritually?

19. What are the Seven Spirits of God?

20. In scripture, does the word "death" mean one can be spiritually separated from God but not "physically dead"?
    TRUE   FALSE

21. Are the Feast classified as Passover, Pentecost, and Tabernacle?
    TRUE   FALSE

22. What day is the "holiest day" out of God's appointed seasons?

23. What are the Seven Blessings of Atonement?

24. What are some of the areas in life we may encounter affliction?
    A. Family   B. Work
    C. Finances   D. Marriage
    E. Children   F. All of the above

25. Is the forgiveness of others the greatest gift you can give to yourself?
    TRUE   FALSE

26. Can Satan impersonate mankind?
    TRUE   FALSE

27. What is the "main negative characteristic" the enemy wants mankind to experience and why?

28. Why does Satan attack the "mind" of mankind?

29. Can the enemy influence someone who is saved?
    TRUE   FALSE

30. Can the enemy have "complete control" over someone who is not saved?
    TRUE   FALSE

31. What are the three ultimate goals of Satan in the destruction of mankind?

32. What does the number "six" mean spiritually?

33. What do we have over the enemy to defeat him every time?
    A. The Father as our Banner,   B. Dominion and Authority
       Jesus and the Holy
       Spirit as our advocate.
    C. The Word of God   D. Weapons of Warfare
    E. Guardian Angels   F. All of the above

34. Does scripture say, "God will never leave you nor forsake you?"
    TRUE   FALSE

35. Have we been rescued from the domain of darkness and soon God will crush Satan under our feet?
    TRUE   FALSE

36. Can the Bully be defeated when you know who are and what you possess!
    TRUE   FALSE

37. What is a Tallit? What spiritual covering does it possess, and where does it take you?

Final Exam Answer Key

1. Did God instruct us, "to seek His kingdom first?
    TRUE FALSE

2. Is God a God of order, cycles, seasons, and principles?
    TRUE FALSE

3. Are we supposed to take everything to the Lord in prayer?
    TRUE FALSE

4. Is tithing in the kingdom of God like an investment, and God promises a lucrative return, an abundance of blessings?
    TRUE FALSE

5. In scripture God quotes, that if we don't have _____ it's impossible to please Him?
    A. Freedom   B. Focus
    C. Friends   ***D. Faith***
    E. All of the Above

6. What should we do with the Word of God day and night to be prosperous?
    Mediate on it

7. Is it crucial that we write down our visions and dreams?
    TRUE FALSE

8. Does Scripture tell us confession is good for our souls?
   TRUE   FALSE

9. What is the Agreement Principle?
   Two are better than one and if two agree on asking anything, it shall be done.

10. Can people perish from lack of knowledge?
    TRUE   FALSE

11. Where should we place the Mezuzah and what is its symbolic purpose?
    We place it upon the doorpost of our homes and God promises that he will protect our travels going out and coming in.

12. Is fasting a principle?
    TRUE   FALSE

13. What does the bread and wine symbolize for Holy Communion?
    Both are sacrificial, the bread represents the body of Jesus Christ and the wine is the shedding of His blood.

14. Does scripture tell us to pray continually?
    TRUE   FALSE

15. What are the Seven Principles within the Lord's Prayer?
    Honor, Confession, Agreement, Repentance, Forgiveness, Rebuking the enemy, and Praise and Worship

16. Explain the Expectation Principle?
    When we pray to the Father, expect Him to bless us, stay in faith

17. Which terms describe "Patience"?
    A. Longsuffering   B. Delay
    C. Tolerance   D. Peace
    E. All of the Above

18. What does the number "Seven" mean spiritually?
    Perfection and Completion

19. What are the Seven Spirits of God?
    Love, Righteousness, Knowledge, Wisdom, Faith, Hope, and Judgment

20. In scripture, does the word "death" mean one can be spiritually separated from God but not "physically dead"?
    TRUE   FALSE

21. Are the Feast classified as Passover, Pentecost and Tabernacle?
    TRUE   FALSE

22. What day is the "holiest day" out of God's appointed seasons?
    The Day of Atonement/ Yom Kippur

23. What are the Seven Blessings of Atonement?
    A Double Portion, Financial Abundance, Restoration, Miracles, Gods Divine Presence, Blessings upon Family, and Deliverance

24. What are some of the areas in life, we may encounter affliction?
    A. Family   B. Work
    C. Finances   D. Marriage
    E. Children   **_F. All of the Above_**

25. Is the forgiveness of others, the greatest gift you can give to yourself?
    TRUE   FALSE

26. Can Satan impersonate mankind?
TRUE   FALSE

27. What is the "main negative characteristic" the Enemy wants mankind to experience and why?
Fear, because when we are in fear we are not trusting God . . .

28. Why does Satan attack the "Mind" of mankind?
Because the mind controls both the body and soul of mankind and Satan is trying to destroy mankind's mind, body and soul and in return it paralyzes our Spirit man.

29. Can the Enemy influence someone who is saved?
TRUE   FALSE

30. Can the Enemy have "complete control" over someone who is not saved?
TRUE   FALSE

31. What are the three ultimate goals of Satan in the destruction of mankind?
To rob, kill and destroy mankind

32. What does the number "six" mean spiritually?
Man

33. What do we have over the Enemy to defeat him every time?
A. The Father as our Banner, Jesus and the Holy Spirit as our advocate.   B. Dominion and Authority
C. The Word of God   D. Weapons of Warfare
E. Guardian Angels   *F. All of the Above*

34. Does scripture say, God will never leave you nor forsake you?
TRUE   FALSE

35. Have we been rescued from the domain of darkness and soon God will crush Satan under our feet?
    TRUE   FALSE

36. Can the "Bully" be defeated when you know who are, and what you possess!
    TRUE   FALSE

37. What is a Tallit? What spiritual covering does it possess and where does it take you?

    A tallit is a prayer shawl. It protects the mind during prayer from the enemy, when we cover our heads with it during prayer we enter into what is spiritually discerned as the "secrete place" and the enemy cannot intercept on our prayers.

The Names of God Cross Word Puzzles

God knows us by our name. Shouldn't we know Him by His?

"You must not misuse the name of the Lord your
God. The Lord will not let you go unpunished
if you misuse his name." (Deut. 5:11)

Name:_____ Date: _____

The Names of God

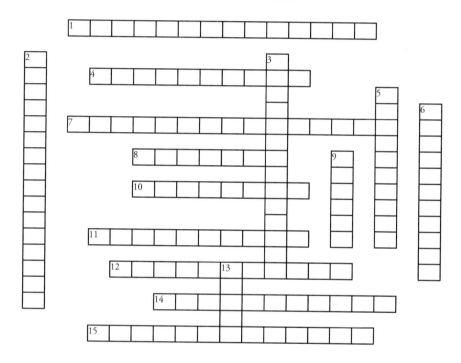

Across
1 YESHUA HAMASHIACH
4 JEHOVAH - MOSHI'ECH
7 JEHOVAH - RAPHA
8 JEHOVAH-'ORI
10 JEHOVAH- NISSA
11 JEHOVAH - ROHI
12 JEHOVAH- MEKODDISHKEM
14 JEHOVAH-MELECH'OLAM
15 JEHOVAH - SABAOTH

Down
2 JEHOVAH - TSIDKENU
3 JEHOVAH-ADON KAL HA'ARETS
5 JEHOVAH - UZI
6 JEHOVAH - MEPHALTI
9 JEHOVAH - SEL'I
13 JEHOVAH - ELI

Name:_____ Date: _____

The Names of God

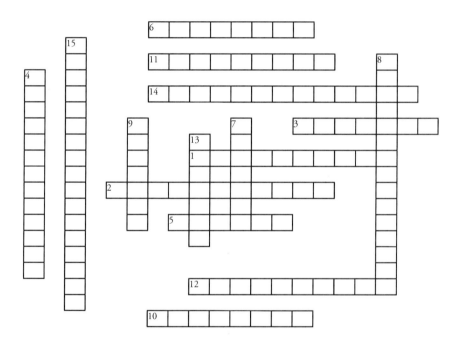

Across
1 EL-OLAM
2 EL-SHADDAI
3 JEHOVAH
5 JEHOVAH-ELOHENU
6 JEHOVAH-GO'EL
10 JEHOVAH-MACHSI
11 JEHOVAH-MAGEN
12 JEHOVAH-MA'OZI
14 JEHOVAH-MAKEH

Down
4 JEHOVAH-CHEREB
7 JEHOVAH-HAMELECH
8 JEHOVAH-HOSHE'AH
9 JEHOVAH-KABODHI
13 EL-KANNA
15 JEHOVAH-KEREN-YISH'I

Name:_____Date: _____

The Names of God

Across
2 EL
3 ALPHA AND OMEGA
4 ADONAI
6 JEHOVAH-SHAMMA
8 YHWH
9 ELOHIM
10 EL-ROI
11 EL-ELYON
14 JEHOVAH-JIREH

Down
1 THE MESSIAH
5 JEHOVAH-SHALOM
7 ABBA
12 JEHOVAH-HASHOPET
13 JEHOVAH-'IZUZ 'GIBBOR
15 JEHOVAH-HOSHE'AH

The Names of God

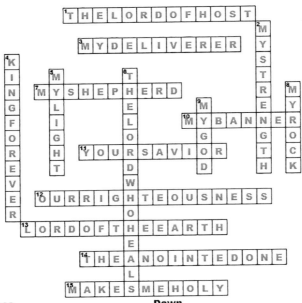

Across
1. JEHOVAH - SABAOTH
3. JEHOVAH - MEPHALTI
7. JEHOVAH - ROHI
10. JEHOVAH- NISSA
11. JEHOVAH - MOSHI'ECH
12. JEHOVAH - TSIDKENU
13. JEHOVAH-ADON KAL
HA'ARETS
14. YESHUA HAMASHIACH
15. JEHOVAH- MEKODDISHKEM

Down
2. JEHOVAH - UZI
4. JEHOVAH-MELECH'OLAM
5. JEHOVAH-'ORI
6. JEHOVAH - RAPHA
8. JEHOVAH - SEL'I
9. JEHOVAH - ELI

The Names of God

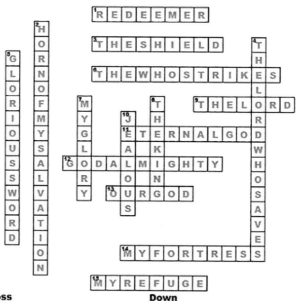

Across
1. JEHOVAH-GO'EL
3. JEHOVAH -MAGEN
6. JEHOVAH- MAKEH
9. JEHOVAH
11. EL-OLAM
12. EL-SHADDAI
13. JEHOVAH -ELOHENU
14. JEHOVAH-MA'OZI
15. JEHOVAH-MACHSI

Down
2. JEHOVAH - KEREN - YISH'I
4. JEHOVAH - HOSHE'AH
5. JEHOVAH-CHEREB
7. JEHOVAH - KABODHI
8. JEHOVAH -HAMELECH
10. EL - KANNA

The Names of God

Across

5. EL
6. YHWH
7. ADONAI
8. ALPHA AND OMEGA
10. ELOHIM
12. EL -ROI
13. EL - ELYON
14. JEHOVAH - JIREH
15. JEHOVAH - SHAMMA

Down

1. JEHOVAH - HOSHE'AH
2. JEHOVAH-'IZUZ 'GIBBOR
3. ABBA
4. JEHOVAH -HASHOPET
9. JEHOVAH - SHALOM
11. THE MESSIAH

About the Author

Lisa Ulmer is a teacher, entrepreneur, and personal motivator. Servicing urban public education, K-12, over the past twenty years, she instructed sociology at the higher education level, possesses undergraduate Degrees in Human Social Services, Psychology and she is a Magna Cum Laude Masters graduate in the field of Education.

Lisa is on a mission to educate and empower believers as well as the unbeliever through practical, biblical, and instructional teaching. Demonstrating a message of expectation, truth and purpose that can apply to everyday life; manifesting wholeness, gaining revelation, free of fear and doubt. Start to walk out your true destiny filled with blessings and miracles.